FDR and the Press

Arthur Mann, Advisory Editor in American History

FDR and the Press

GRAHAM J. WHITE

The University of Chicago Press
Chicago and London

The University of Chicago Press, Chicago 60637
The University of Chicago Press, Ltd., London

© 1979 by The University of Chicago
All rights reserved. Published 1979

Printed in the United States of America
83 82 81 80 79   5 4 3 2 1

GRAHAM J. WHITE is a lecturer in American history
at the University of Sydney.

Illustrations courtesy of the archives
of the Chicago *Tribune.*

Library of Congress Cataloging in Publication Data

White, Graham J
   FDR and the press.

   Revision of the author's thesis, University of Sydney,
1977.
   Bibliography: p.
   Includes index.
   1. United States—Politics and government—1933–1945.
2. Roosevelt, Franklin Delano, Pres. U.S., 1882–1945.
3. Government and the press—United States.   I. Title.
E806.W456   320.9'73'0917   78–11423
ISBN 0-226-89512-2

Contents

Preface

Most of those who have attempted to analyze Franklin Roosevelt have
felt obliged to emphasize the complexities and ambiguities of his character. They have seen in their subject a confusing mixture of puzzling
contradictions: a Hudson River aristocrat turned democrat; a pros-
perous, landed conservative who practiced radicalism; a sworn up-
holder of the Constitution who struck at the Supreme Court; and their
conclusions have been, in so many words, that Franklin Roosevelt was
an enigma, an endless riddle, or, in any event, a man whom it is quite
impossible to understand in any relatively simple or straightforward
manner. Nor could these conclusions be considered surprising. Who, it
might fairly be asked, having examined Franklin Roosevelt's political
record, could throw a mantle of consistency over his aims and actions,
or, by discovering some hidden order in that chaos of improvisation
and experimentation called the New Deal, see clearly into the mind of
its chief architect? Even if Franklin Roosevelt was not ideologically
homeless, an adroit but completely rudderless improviser, should he
not be seen essentially as a pragmatist who, taking his main cues from
changing circumstances and opportunities, merely raked together some
scraps of ideology to bolster his often bewilderingly inconsistent actions? A substantial body of critical opinion would suggest that he
should.[1]

Yet there are grounds for suspecting that the emphasis on the elements of paradox and discontinuity in Franklin Roosevelt may have been
carried far enough. To begin with an obvious question, if Roosevelt was,
as is so frequently argued, without clear direction, conscious of his inconsistencies, deeply divided, as at least one writer has suggested,[2]

between conflicting worlds and experiences, and therefore, presumably, subject to the mental and emotional discomfort with which one might expect such dissonance to be associated, how then does one account for the most conspicuous of all his personality traits—his soaring self-confidence? He, at least, it might be observed, never appeared to have shared the difficulties of those who have been unable to discover in his programs or ideas much evidence of ideological or political consistency. On the contrary, Franklin Roosevelt gave the strong impression that he knew precisely what he was trying to do and, in the process, exuded the kind of confidence which a priori we would not expect a man afflicted with chronic doubts over his identity, political role, or objectives to display. Indeed no impression derived from the present study is stronger than that, in relation to the world of politics at least, Franklin Roosevelt possessed a deeply ingrained positive self-concept; that, in other words, he looked upon himself and upon his role with evident, enduring, and almost total satisfaction. These observations do not sit happily alongside interpretations which depict Roosevelt as a double-minded or philosophically nebulous man.

Admittedly the question may be largely one of balance and degree. It is not so much that one would wish to dispute the basic point that Roosevelt was a highly complex person; it is, rather, that one would want to ask whether this is necessarily the most important point and whether, in discussions of Roosevelt's character, it may not have been emphasized in such a way as to conceal or at least to minimize what may be of greater ultimate significance—the high degree of coherence and consistency, and even a certain simplicity in the man. It is not, therefore, that one need necessarily emphasize his complexity less, but that one might profitably emphasize his simplicity more.

An examination of Franklin Roosevelt's relations with the American press highlights this very point by demonstrating that his essential attitudes toward that institution were derived from a basic and coherent set of assumptions and ideas about American politics and government which he had developed by early 1925 and from whose basic tenets he never departed. Central to this cluster of ideas were an elementary theory of human nature, a simple dualistic notion of social and political conflict resting upon it, a cyclical view of history which saw the control of government alternating between the Jeffersonian "many" and the Hamiltonian "few," and an ideal construct of a democratic state which had been approximated during Jeffersonian booms of the past and which, presumably, would endure if ever the periodic and regrettable slumps into Hamiltonian oligarchic control could be eliminated in the future. In this general connection, no idea was more important than Roosevelt's perception of himself as another Jefferson whose task it was to preserve American democracy against the recurring attempts by Hamiltonian minorities to wrest control of it from the people. All history, to Franklin Roosevelt, was the history of such democratic struggles. Roosevelt's consistency can be appreciated once it is realized that, having developed these ideas early in his career, he spent the rest of his political life spinning out their implications in various spheres. Their importance to him was profound. Unoriginal and banal though they may have been, they nevertheless assumed, once Roosevelt had built them into a structured and integrated system, an intellectual and moral dynamism of their own. Armed with them, he was untroubled by any doubts as to either his long-term purpose or his short-term role. More than this, his self-concept, in political terms, was a profoundly satisfying one, enabling him to identify himself with great presidents of the past, and to see himself as engaged in the same titanic struggle, victory in which had established their greatness. In much the same way he could effectively rationalize and deal with opposition to his policies, overcome the disadvantages of his patrician background, and credibly pose as champion of the people. Franklin Roosevelt's Jeffersonianism had, for him, the comprehensiveness, the assurance, the sense of transcending purpose of a religious faith. Roosevelt's massive self-confidence, it is suggested, was not unrelated to his acceptance of such ideas. Nor, it will be demonstrated, were his basic attitudes toward the press, about which he had, by the time he became president, developed firm expectations both as to its necessary role in an ideal democratic system and as to its historically established tendency during previous periods of democratic trial. Indeed, it was just because, in an important sense, the critique which Franklin Roosevelt applied to the press was ideologically based, inflexible, resistant to fresh evidence, that he became, for that institution, such a formidable and baffling opponent: his battles with it were fought within a frame of historical and ideological reference which its members could only partly understand and under rules which often they could only dimly perceive. For while Roosevelt may have been clear as to its required role and standards, to the press that role seemed unreasonably circumscribed, those standards often arbitrary and irrelevant. What will be demonstrated, however, is that once Roosevelt's basic philosophical and ideological position is appreciated, many aspects of his relations with the press which may have appeared not merely complex but inexplicable fall satisfactorily into place, a proposition which will be recognized as having a more general implication.

On one level, the outcome of this inquiry should be to help set straight the record concerning the press's treatment of Franklin Roosevelt and to clear away some myths behind which this subject has been partially obscured. More significantly, this research constitutes an extended study, not hitherto attempted, of one facet of the life of a highly important political figure. It is one thing to recognize, as many have, that Franklin Roosevelt displayed a degree of virtuosity in his handling and his exploitation of the press which was (and is) probably unsurpassed; it is another to construct a sustained analysis to demonstrate why this was so, and thus to illuminate, so far as Franklin Roosevelt was concerned, one area in which his extraordinary political skill can be seen to full advantage. But, ultimately, this study constitutes an attempt to interpret Franklin Roosevelt in a new way. His imagined political affinity with Thomas Jefferson, his familiarity with the notion of an inherent antagonism and continuing struggle between antidemocratic Hamiltonian minorities and Jeffersonian majorities (which, after all, formed part of the intellectual baggage of the Progressive era) may have been recognized; the centrality of their importance, so far as Franklin Roosevelt is concerned, has not. What is here demonstrated, through detailed study of his relations with the press, is that his commitment to these ideas—certainly superficial, possibly delusive—exerted a basic, even a controlling influence over Franklin Roosevelt's attitudes and his behavior; what is implied is that a recognition of Roosevelt's commitment to these ideas may be of considerable assistance in explaining his behavior in other areas. In short, the argument to be developed in the following pages constitutes an attempt to clear away the ambiguities and supposed complexities which surround Franklin Roosevelt's political personality and to discover the rock upon which the edifice of his political life was built.

The major conclusions of this research bear on another broad issue. One question which has exercised both contemporaries and historians concerns the place of the New Deal in the American political tradition and, more specifically, whether it represented a major discontinuity, which, breaking sharply with the past, shifted the American political, social, and economic system in new, and, to some, alien directions. Had Franklin Roosevelt, when he gave the American people a new deal, merely reshuffled the existing political, economic, and philosophical cards, or had he used a different pack? The interpretation of Franklin Roosevelt presented in these pages makes it clear that, in the eyes of its chief architect at least, any "newness" in the New Deal related essentially to the means by which the latest in a long series of attempts by minority groups to wrest control of the American system from the people had been turned back, the essentially conservative end of his policies never being in doubt.

This study began and ended with the Roosevelt press conferences. From them came, directly or indirectly, its initial questions and its main controlling ideas; against the evidence contained in them solutions were tested, ideas modified and developed. The unique importance of the press conferences is that they enable Roosevelt to speak for himself, to reveal his mind. In the course of more than five million words, by rough estimate, of press conference transcript, in spontaneous answer to all manner of questions, impromptu lecture, gratuitous comment, or through sheer inadvertence, one learns his views—on the Washington press corps, on publishers, on the press's ethics, its failings, its function, ideally, with the American governmental system. Without necessarily accepting what Roosevelt says at face value, one is nevertheless in a position to begin to study Franklin Roosevelt from the standpoint of what he says about himself and his beliefs about what he is like. If answers are not always given, certain questions are insistently posed.

Apart from the extensive use made of the presidential press conference, this study of Franklin Roosevelt's relations with the press is grounded on an analysis of certain unpublished material held at the Franklin D. Roosevelt Library, Hyde Park, New York, particularly the papers of Roosevelt himself and of his press secretary Stephen Early, but including, also, those of Samuel I. Rosenman, William D. Hassett, Lowell Mellett, and the records of the Democratic National Committee. At the Library of Congress, Washington, D.C., the papers of William Allen White, Harold L. Ickes, Raymond Clapper, Helen Rogers Reid, Victor Murdock, and Joseph and Stewart Alsop were consulted; from the Lilly Library, Indiana University, a portion of the papers of Claude G. Bowers was obtained. Other important sources from which information was derived were several of the interviews conducted in connection with the Columbia University Oral History Project, and a very large number of contemporary newspapers, magazines, and journals. Naturally, much of this material has been scrutinized by others (though some of it, notably the very extensive analyses of newspaper treatment of the New Deal supplied to the president by the Division of Press Intelligence, I suspect, has not); but it has been examined by those with other purposes in mind, without the material ever being, where it concerned the president's relations with individual newspaper owners, columnists, or reporters, exploited in full, or without it ever having been drawn together for general evaluation and analysis. In relation to the use to which material from these sources has previously been put, it could be pointed out, further, that while Franklin Roosevelt's relations with the press have briefly been looked at as constituting one aspect of his presidency, his presidency has not been approached from the vantage point of an analysis of his relations with the press.

In connection with this study I received generous financial assistance, for which I am grateful, from the University of Sydney, by way of an Overseas Travel Grant, and from the Eleanor Roosevelt Foundation. I am appreciative, also, of the efforts of the staffs of various libraries. To my many requests, often unusual, for assistance, the staff of the Franklin D. Roosevelt Library, Hyde Park, New York, have responded with courtesy, promptness, and great efficiency; my debt to them is considerable. Similarly, the staff of the Library of Congress and the National Records Center at Washington, the Lilly Library, Indiana

University, and the New York Public Library have been unfailingly helpful and also exceedingly efficient. To the staffs of Fisher Library, University of Sydney, and Monash University Library, Victoria, also go my thanks.

I am grateful, too, for the assistance which I have received from several individuals. Professor Saul Padover of the New School of Social Research, New York, a participator in the events about which I have written, apart from sharing with me some personal information relating to the period of my research, expressed great interest in my topic, pointed me in several fruitful directions, and made helpful comments about my methodological approach in the area of newspaper sampling. Professor Arthur Mann of the University of Chicago has encouraged me, discussed my ideas, and given much sagacious advice. I am particularly indebted, too, to Dr. Lazar Stankov of the Department of Psychology in the University of Sydney, whose main expertise lies in the statistical field, because he has been prepared, in broad terms, to put the seal of his approval on the procedures which I have devised for finding answers to certain specific questions relating to Franklin Roosevelt's treatment at the hands of the press, and, over several discussions, has helped me both to refine those procedures and more carefully and accurately to spell out the implications of the results which they produced. To my father, who has patiently corrected the proofs of this work and made useful suggestions concerning the organization of the material, I am also grateful. Finally, I wish to express my thanks to Dr. Christiana M. Campbell of the Department of History in the University of Sydney. It was she who suggested a topic which I have found to be rich and significant, who assisted me, too, with criticism and advice. She has also, by her outlook and her approach to the study of history itself, helped materially to make the experience of producing this book not merely satisfying, but also enjoyable.

Introduction

Franklin Roosevelt's account of his relations with the press was brief and unvarying. The simple thesis which he propagated tirelessly throughout his presidency was that the press opposed him; that its opposition was proprietor-based; and that he was confronted, as a result of such hostility, not merely with widespread editorial disapproval, but with tendentious and distorted news reports. A long footnote to the transcript of his first presidential press conference, as reprinted in the 1938 edition of his *Public Papers and Addresses*, became the authorized public version of such views.[1]

Roosevelt had no doubts either as to the magnitude of press opposition to his administration, or the menacing nature of the proprietors who directed it. The opposition of the press was overwhelming, with 85 percent of the nation's newspapers antagonistic toward the New Deal. As to the owners of what Roosevelt collectively dubbed "the Tory press," their backgrounds were dubious, their journalistic talents meager, and their motives suspect. Products largely of the counting room rather than the news desk, such men could not distinguish between "an objective news story and a free reader for a furniture store";[2] yet, so great was the measure of their control, the press reflected their standards and purveyed their prejudices. Even where they had risen through the ranks of journalism, newspaper proprietors were imperiled by the very nature of their occupation: once they reached a certain level of affluence they embraced the Hamiltonian theory of society and government, and "the check book and the securities market supplant[ed] the old patriotism and the old desire to purvey straight news to the public."[3] To Franklin Roosevelt the power of such newspaper owners, excessive and unmerited, constituted a threat not merely to press freedom, but to democracy itself. The nation's reporters, by contrast, were in a subservient and ineffectual position. Though pro-administration in their sympathies and more than adequate in their professional capabilities, they were reluctantly forced, often on pain of dismissal, to conform to the owners' "personal slant." "I understand," Roosevelt remarked characteristically at a press conference on 9 August 1937, "You fellows are placed in such a position very often.... I can appreciate what you are told to write."

Roosevelt's admiration for the working press was not unqualified. Most obviously it stopped well short of the nation's columnists, who, he believed, based most of their writing on imagination or gossip, frequently tailored their output to the needs of their clients, and who, as a consequence, were regarded by their readers with tolerant amusement, by their colleagues with professional disdain, and by the president, it was obvious, with lofty contempt. To be a reporter was an honorable occupation; to be a columnist, a disgrace.

Time and again, often under circumstances which belie the suggestion that his remarks were designed solely for public consumption or narrow political advantage, Roosevelt recorded these basic convictions about the press. Throughout a long presidency he would neither modify them in the face of evidence, nor develop them in the light of experience. But though his attitude may have been obdurate, his reluctance is not surprising; to Franklin Roosevelt such propositions were axiomatic.

This study uses the central propositions of Roosevelt's critique of the press, as they relate to reporters, proprietors, press opposition, and news distortion, as a loose analytical and organizational framework within which the president's relations with that institution are discussed.

Chapters 1 and 2 are devoted to a consideration of Roosevelt's relations with the Washington correspondents, with emphasis being given to the president's spectacular initial victory over the press corps, the longer-term bases of his popularity, the remarkably skillful manner in which he was able, by his adroit handling of the reporters, to use the press to his own political advantage, and the often serious conflict which occurred between the president and the correspondents. Always underlying and sometimes disturbing the pattern of interaction between Roosevelt and the Washington reporters was the president's highly circumscribed conception of the role of the press and a related set of expectations regarding the reporters' functions which they, as a group, were unwilling to fulfill.

Chapter 3 examines the anatomy of Roosevelt's relations with the newspaper owners in order, primarily, to demonstrate that the president's comprehensive denunciations of newspaper owners as a group cannot be reconciled with his dealings with a not insignificant number of owners as individuals.

Chapters 4 and 5 are concerned with the treatment of Franklin Roosevelt by the press, and, more specifically, with an evaluation of Roosevelt's charges that the overwhelming majority of the press was against him, and that many hostile newspaper owners forced their reporter-employees to "slant" their dispatches against Roosevelt's administration. The validity of both charges is strongly questioned.

In chapter 6, the discontinuities, which have emerged in preceding chapters, between Roosevelt's statements about the press and his actual relations with it, together with certain other distinctive attitudes manifested by the president toward that institution, are highlighted, and, in the final chapter, synthesized and explained in terms of Franklin Roosevelt's Jeffersonian political philosophy.

One

FIRESIDE MATHEMATICS

The Best Newspaperman Who Has Ever Been
President of the United States

The initial victory of Franklin Roosevelt over the Washington press was swift and glorious. Demonstrating a virtuosity that amazed them, the new president took the Capital correspondents by storm, winning, from the outset, their affection and admiration; securing, over the crucial early stages of the New Deal, their allegiance and support. The correspondents themselves have amply recorded his triumph: his first meeting with the reporters, said one, was "the most amazing performance the White House has ever seen"; he quickly won from the newsmen, observed another, their friendship and "what cooperation they can give consistent with covering the news—which is quite a lot"; he was, declared a third, "a great hit among the newspapermen at Washington." Comments on his impact became effusive:

> I rubbed my ears [wrote newsman Marlen Pew] and opened my eyes when I heard hard-boiled veterans, men who had lived through so many administrations that there are callouses in their brain, talk glibly about the merits of the White House incumbent.[1]

The accolades continued throughout the president's first year: in June, Arthur Sears Henning, a Washington newsman for twenty-three years and chief of the *Chicago Tribune*'s Washington bureau for nineteen years, estimated that the relationship between the White House and the press had never been as satisfactory from the newspapermen's point of view;[2] "the reportorial affection and admiration" for the president, declared Raymond Tucker, in the October edition of *Collier's* was "unprecedented." "He has," Tucker stated, "definitely captivated an unusually cynical battalion of correspondents."

Traditionally, presidential honeymoons with the Washington press had been brief, but in the June 1934 issue of *Review of Reviews* Raymond Clapper drew attention to the continuing Roosevelt press triumph: "Mr. Roosevelt...came to Washington. The correspondents saw him and were conquered. He won them and he has still a larger proportion of them personally sympathetic than any of his recent predecessors." A year later, a front-page editorial in *Scoop*, the annual publication of the Press Club of San Francisco, enthusiastically reiterated the point:

> This edition of the annual *Scoop* we dedicate to the "best news source in America," Franklin D. Roosevelt.... the nation's reporters will smile contentedly as long as F.R. sits on the throne dishing out "hot copy."... Instead of dreading a boring White House press conference, they now look forward to these gatherings with enthusiasm.
> The Press Club of San Francisco salutes you, F.R.[3]

What lay behind this unprecedented newspaper success? To the Washington reporters, it is clear, Roosevelt's virtues were etched vividly against the somber background of his predecessors' incompetence. Before becoming president, Herbert Hoover had been popular with the Washington correspondents, and in the three months following his inauguration his press conferences were rich and useful. Yet, by October 1931, journalist Paul Anderson could write that Hoover's relations with the reporters had "reached a state of unpleasantness without parallel during the present century."[4]

The history of the transformation is instructive. Hoover angered the reporters by playing favorites, was inconsiderate of their needs, and reacted to criticism at first with sensitivity and later with vindictiveness. More fundamentally, he forfeited popularity by permitting the quality and quantity of presidential news to decline. Economic circumstances were partly to blame: as the depression deepened, so did Hoover's gloom, and, making fewer efforts to overcome his lack of loquacity, he dried up as a news source. In the face of his sullen aridity, press relations withered.

It was against this gloomy and unproductive background that Frank-

lin Roosevelt's virtues shone forth with a clear and penetrating brilliance. His manner, when he met the press, was candid and friendly;
his answers quick and illuminating; and the depression which had so
burdened his predecessor seemed to have left his confidence and
buoyancy unaffected. Journalistic egos were soothed by Roosevelt's
affable and colloquial manner; professional pride appeased by his clear
recognition of the importance of the reporters' role. Especially dramatic was the new president's announcement that he would abolish the
written-questions rule, a practice which had prevailed since an addled
or ignorant Warren Harding, attempting an off-the-cuff answer to a
reporter's query, committed a diplomatic faux pas which mortified his
secretary of state and embarrassed his government. Where written
questions were demanded, the initiative in press conferences lay firmly
with the president, who could ignore awkward questions altogether, or
deliver propaganda in the guise of answers to questions which had
never been asked. Roosevelt's daring innovation signaled his intention
to meet the reporters on equal terms, to subject himself to the scrutiny
of the entire press corps when he reacted to its queries. For the press, as
for the people, the "New Deal" had begun.

Under Roosevelt, what had been a pitiful trickle of White House
news increased to a torrent. In his first press conference, one correspondent estimated, the new president produced more sensational
news than some of his predecessors had released in four years. By
comparison with Franklin Roosevelt, "all previous Presidents were
Trappists who didn't even talk to themselves." [5]

Such comparisons were multiplied. Unlike Hoover, the new incumbent provided for the reporters' comfort on presidential trips,
seemed positively to enjoy their company, and showed a keen understanding of journalistic psychology. The contrast with Woodrow Wilson was equally vivid. Like Roosevelt, he had evinced a determination
to publicize government affairs, but while the end was admirable the
means were frequently abrasive. Lacking Roosevelt's intuitive understanding of the journalists' needs, Wilson prepared for his press conferences as carefully as for any lecture, talked to the press like a
schoolmaster, resented being cross-examined by a group whom he
considered his intellectual inferiors, and became irritated when the

questioning moved in personal or trivial directions. Aloof, humorless, and suspicious, he was unable ever to establish that rapport with the correspondents which was to be the hallmark of Franklin Roosevelt's success.[6]

Roosevelt won additional credit for not launching "trial balloons," as some previous incumbents, notably Calvin Coolidge, had done. Because Coolidge refused to be quoted on, or accept responsibility for, any statement which he made, reporters invented a mythical "White House spokesman," whose dubious authority, they hoped, would bolster their dispatches. Coolidge then used this spectral figure to launch trial balloons, disclaiming responsibility if the balloons blew in politically embarrassing directions. As frustration mounted, reporters took to referring to Coolidge's press conferences as "seances," and an exasperated editor finally denounced them as "symposia of silliness" which had been "reduced to the lowest point of futility."[7]

Coolidge did earn a measure of grudging respect. The Washington press regarded him as an urbane and canny New Englander, an accomplished politician, an artful publicist, but an inveterate twaddler, who raised the practice of disseminating trivia almost to an art form. On matters of substance, on the other hand, his remarks were timid, nebulous, and inconsistent. Denied solid news, the reporters turned to myth, attempting through their dispatches to impart color and news value to a man who naturally possessed neither. But with Franklin Roosevelt, who provided the correspondents with a continuous supply of "live" news stories, and who electrified them with his dynamism and astonished them with the scope of his action, such dissimulation was never necessary.

In the June 1934 issue of *Review of Reviews*, Raymond Clapper, United Press bureau chief in Washington, wove many of these points into an analysis of the reasons for Roosevelt's unusual and continuing popularity. Clapper emphasized the pleasantness of the reporters' routine contacts with the president, the hospitality he extended to them, the fact that he was willing, on such informal occasions, to discuss confidential policies with them long before publication was permitted. Then, too, Roosevelt's press conferences were invariably productive of news, a circumstance linked by Clapper to the president's decision to abandon the written-questions rule and to assume full responsibility for his answers. Additionally, the reporters respected Roosevelt's political craftsmanship, sympathized with his objectives, and admired his courage.

Clapper's list should be extended. Franklin Roosevelt's superb insight into publicity techniques, his "news sense," his ability to time releases so that they achieved maximum impact, and his rare talent for dramatizing his actions and announcements, imparting distinctive news value even to routine affairs, earned the admiration, as well as the gratitude, of professionals.[8] So did his capacity to give the reporters information in a form suitable for incorporation into their dispatches. "Every newspaperman who has attended his press conferences," wrote correspondent Ernest Lindley, "knows his gift for simple and logical analysis. He accumulates masses of detail but he can cut through them to the heart of the problem."[9] Such abilities were especially valued in the early New Deal period, for, not only was the pace of events frantic, but the entire character of news seemed to have changed. Leo Rosten's extensive interviews and informal contacts with more than 150 members of the Washington press corps over a fourteen-month period during Roosevelt's first term convinced him that a substantial majority of the correspondents felt keenly their inadequacy in the face of events which were not merely unfamiliar but bewilderingly complex.[10] Such apprehension was sometimes reflected in press conference questions: "Off-the-record, Mr. President," one harassed correspondent asked Roosevelt, on 28 July 1933, "can you fill us in on what the situation is on that [the possible inflation of the dollar]? Personally, I am as ignorant as a nincompoop on it all."

The fruits of Franklin Roosevelt's initial victory over the Washington press corps were rich. Such was the charm with which he mesmerized the Capital correspondents that only the most resolute could remain entirely unaffected and many felt themselves losing their cherished ability to scrutinize each new administration with skepticism and objectivity. A representative of *Editor and Publisher*, trade journal of the newspaper industry, who spent a week in December 1934 interviewing twenty-five top reporters, discovered among them a general belief that the Roosevelt personality was leading to the coloration of Washington news stories. Arthur Krock, head of the *New York Times* bureau, lamented the fact that writers were pulling their punches. The chief of another large bureau complained that he was continually receiving letters from editors asking whether the president had the press hamstrung.[11] As late as January 1936, J. Fred Essary, chief of the Washington bureau of the *Baltimore Sun*, found it necessary to make a spirited rejection of the charge that the Washington correspondents had become propagandists for the administration, committed to glorifying the president's acts and purposes.[12] In these early New Deal years, Roosevelt's triumph over the Washington press corps seemed all but complete.

Ultimately, the measure of that triumph lay in the evaluations of the professionals, who judged the president's performance and profited from his skill. Against the practical criteria drawn from their store of experience the new incumbent was assessed. Their verdict was clear-cut and virtually unanimous. Franklin Roosevelt had "the news sense of a managing editor," "might qualify as the chief of a great copy desk," was without peer in his handling of the reporters. Franklin Roosevelt, declared columnist Heywood Broun, delivering the final accolade, was "the best newspaperman who has even been President of the United States."[13]

The structure of Roosevelt's relations with the Washington press, which had been erected with skill, was maintained with resolution. Throughout the entire period of his presidency, the correspondents agreed, Roosevelt's contacts with the press were pleasant, his news output abundant; and, among the Capital newsmen with whom he dealt, his expertise was respected, his impartiality acknowledged, and his popularity, as a consequence, substantially undiminished. Recurring controversy might shake, but could not destroy, these foundations.

The record of continuing pleasantness in the contacts between Roosevelt and the Washington press can be traced in the transcripts of the press conferences and the tributes of the correspondents. The tone of the opening exchanges at a press conference on 11 October 1933, was not uncharacteristic:

Q: Good morning, Mr. President.
The President: Good morning. (Exhibiting saber)
Q: Are you going to cut off a few heads this morning?

The President: ...Charlie (Mr. Hurd), you have to be good this
morning. You watch your questions carefully....
Q: Anything about the monetary situation? (Asked by Mr.
Hurd) *The President:* Give me that sword. (Laughter)

Such jovial informality continued to draw appreciative comment:
never before, observed one member of the press corps in December
1936, had routine associations between president and press been
more agreeable; Franklin Roosevelt, declared its most senior member,
in March 1937, was "the most amiable Oval Room leader within
memory."[14]

More was involved here than political calculation. Though Roosevelt
courted the reporters openly and cultivated them as a group, his
affection for them, they could not but realize, was deep and unfeigned.
Far from being a burdensome chore, press conferences were stimulating and enjoyable interludes, to which Roosevelt looked forward, in
the later estimation of one newsman, with the same enthusiasm with
which Dwight Eisenhower contemplated a game of golf.[15] His affectionate regard for the reporters was evidenced, too, by his constant
attendance at their functions and the manner in which he publicly
championed their cause. But more revealing still were the extraordinarily generous compliments he occasionally paid, of which none was
more remarkable than a tribute published by *Collier's* in January 1945.
Dedicated by Roosevelt to "the reporter," and given by him to the
editor of the magazine some years earlier, it read:

He is everywhere.
His perception, his intelligence, encompass all men, all things,
[*sic*] His eye scans the earth, surveying its tragedies and comedies,
its men of wealth and of poverty.
In the beginning he chiselled in living rock the news of the first
dawns of promise. In the great ending, he will write "thirty"—his
own mystic symbol of conclusion—and the strange history of man
will be complete [*sic*]. . . .

In the light of such sentiments, the Washington correspondents'
references to Franklin Roosevelt as "a reporters' President" and "the
best newspaperman who has ever been President" gain a further
dimension.

Responding to Franklin Roosevelt's goodwill toward them and appreciating his efforts on their behalf, the Washington correspondents repaid him generously in affection and overlooked many of his faults. Roosevelt might attack the reporters, or obstruct them, or display a petulance which might have produced serious alienation, but a permanent falling-away did not occur. A veteran correspondent, a firsthand observer of press relations under four presidents, explained why:

> With Roosevelt, this is the only time that I had the feeling that I was welcome here in the White House, that I belonged here, that I was as important here as a member of Cabinet or of Congress—even more important. I think you'll find that feeling general. . . . here, at Hyde Park and on his special trains, we're not only welcome but we have the distinct feeling—for the first time—that we belong there, that he's *our* President. Ours. See?[16]

Pleasantness and goodwill alone would not have continued to satisfy the Washington correspondents had the output of White House news been inadequate. Under Franklin Roosevelt it rarely was. He met the reporters twice weekly and his conferences with them continued to yield a rich harvest of live news. At these meetings with the press, Roosevelt's knowledge of detail was a continual source of wonder: he could discuss, the reporters discovered, local, national, or international issues with equal assurance and facility. Indeed, for all his adroitness and charm, many reporters found this to be Roosevelt's most impressive quality— the sheer range of his information.

Part of the explanation for this copious news output was essentially personal: Franklin Roosevelt, with his vivid and exciting personality, was fascinating to newsmen. "You are still the most interesting person," William Allen White told him at the annual presidential press conference for news editors in April 1939. "For box office attraction you leave Clark Gable gasping for breath." Roosevelt's capacity for making politics absorbing and vital, his unusual talent for dramatization, and his active presidential style which exploited conflict as a means of publicity—all these produced material which made first-rate news copy.

In contemporary comments on Franklin Roosevelt's relations with

the press, references to the expertise which he displayed in the conduct
of his press conferences are an insistent and recurring theme. "Every
time one goes to a White House press conference," wrote Bulkley
Griffin in the *Hartford Times* of 16 December 1940, "he is made to
recognize once again that Franklin D. Roosevelt is without peer in
meeting newsmen." The president's performance, observers agreed,
was superb, his technique incomparable, and his virtuosity of a kind
that, irrespective of where their basic sympathies lay, the Washington
correspondents could neither fail to benefit from nor cease to admire.

At his meetings with reporters, Roosevelt's expository skill continued
to earn respect. His ability to explain the broad outlines of administration policy in language which the reporters could understand, to use
homely metaphors and salient examples, fitted precisely the reporters'
practical need for speed and simplification, and made their task im-
measurably easier. Nor could they fail to admire the skillful way in
which he retained control. The initiative under the oral questioning
system may have appeared to lie with the reporters; in practice, as they
knew, it rarely passed from Roosevelt's hands. Frequently, he began
his conferences with announcements of such news importance that
those issues dominated the conference and preempted discussion of
more embarrassing questions. Roosevelt had the ability, too, where
questions on them were not forthcoming, to introduce into the body of
a press conference subjects to which he wished prominence to be given.
Evasion presented few problems. Roosevelt could fail to hear a question, or give a facetious answer—as he did when he was asked his
opinion of some charts of economic indicators displayed at a press
conference on 15 November 1933, and replied: "Very nicely done."
Where difficult questions on economic matters were introduced, he
might exploit the reporters' feelings of inadequacy in this area by
reminding them that they belonged to one of the two professions in the
world (the other being the clergy) that did not know the difference
between dollars and dimes; or retreat into pedantic literalism by, for
example, asking a reporter who had raised the question of inflation to
define the concept. Another of his ploys—one which he instructed other
members of the administration to emulate—was to deny knowledge of
the subject of an embarrassing question, even where he possessed it.

Added to all this was the unwritten rule that once Roosevelt had signified his unwillingness to discuss an issue he was not to be pressed. "It is," he assured a press conference with journalism teachers in December 1935, "perfectly easy to avoid telling things you do not want to have come out."

In this general context, the good humor that prevailed in his press conferences was very much to Roosevelt's advantage. Frequently, he could avoid a difficult question with a quip that threw the whole room into laughter—often being abetted by several reporters whose main purpose, in the words of one of their more serious colleagues, "seems to be to say something so cute that the President doubles up with laughter." [17] In either event, before the author of the embarrassing question could follow it up, the conference was likely to have moved off in a different direction.

Presiding over his press conferences, Franklin Roosevelt was compared to a consummate performer, a brilliant and accomplished actor, who met the challenge of a critical audience and took pleasure and pride in his own performance, seldom missing his cues. Like an actor, too, he eagerly asked for critical comment after each performance, and to one whose opinion he habitually sought he undoubtedly owed a large measure of his success.

Stephen Early, Roosevelt's press secretary, had behind him an extensive career in newspaper and newsreel work and a friendship with the president that reached back to Roosevelt's term as assistant secretary of the navy, which Early, as an Associated Press reporter, had been assigned to cover. From that time he had become associated with Roosevelt, Marvin McIntyre, and Louis Howe in a group which met annually to celebrate Roosevelt's birthday and which subsequently became known as the Cuff Links Club. In 1920, Early joined Roosevelt's vice-presidential campaign organization as "advance man," but, following Roosevelt's defeat, rejoined the Washington staff of the Associated Press. In 1927 he became Washington representative of Paramount Newsreel, from which position he was appointed, as also had been the other club members, Howe and McIntyre, to the Roosevelt secretariat.

The selection of Early and two other accomplished newsmen to Roosevelt's personal staff was seen to be auspicious—a clear indication, Washington correspondents thought, of the importance which the new president was preparing to attach with his relations with the press. Early, Howe, and McIntyre, newsman George H. Manning pointed out, were personally well known and liked by most of the correspondents, understood their needs and psychology, and were expected to be extremely useful to them.[18]

In Early's case, Manning's forecast proved accurate: in memoirs, letters, and journalistic literature of the period, generous tribute has been paid to the press secretary's unusual ability, continuing popularity, and professional success. It was Early who originated many of the innovations which cemented Roosevelt's relations with the press. It was he who urged Roosevelt to throw open the doors of his administration to the press, who persuaded him to abandon the written-questions rule, and who cautioned him against treating the reporters with other than complete impartiality. He worked, too, to change the atmosphere of the White House, so that, in his own words, the correspondents would be "welcomed, as gentlemen, not suspected as spies." Early was accessible at any hour of the day or night to reply to reporters' questions, and, what was equally important, knew most of the answers. Nor did he hesitate to confront his superiors to ask for more information. Thus, when Secretary Woodin declined to give the press further details about the new administration's banking program, which was known to have been prepared for submission to Congress, Early went directly to Roosevelt and a more complete statement was quickly forthcoming.[19]

The press secretary's influence extended to every government department and agency, where party hacks in press agents' jobs were replaced by experienced newsmen. The impact of these appointees was often striking: Charles Michelson caused an upheaval in the Treasury by insisting that no statements were to be released to the press unless he, himself, could understand them. Michelson's influence over Treasury Secretary Woodin was equally dramatic: within a fortnight of taking office a man who had begun by being shy and suspicious of newsmen was visiting Treasury press headquarters, and entertaining the delighted reporters with a mandolin version of his latest musical compositions. Only with difficulty did Michelson persuade him against providing a refrigerator filled with beer for his "new friends."[20]

Highly significant, too, was the role which Early played in developing

Roosevelt's press conference technique. Before each conference, he provided the president with newsworthy announcements, anticipated questions he might be asked, and groomed him for suitable replies. At its conclusion, he reviewed Roosevelt's performance and suggested how his technique might be improved.

To the extent to which it was successful, Early's insistence on a policy of evenhanded treatment in White House dealings with the press was an important factor in Roosevelt's continuing popularity. Again and again the press secretary reaffirmed the commitment to that policy, and, by and large, the reporters appear to have believed what he said. "Of one thing I am sure," asserted James L. Wright in 1935, "Mr. Roosevelt has no fair-haired boys who can slip in for a few minutes' private chat and get an exclusive story." Much later, as he looked back over the whole period of Roosevelt's presidency, Charles Hurd was hard-pressed to recall a single occasion on which Roosevelt's particular friends in the newspaper world had been given an advantage over their competitors.[21] Though hostility was aroused by one or two breaches of the policy of impartiality, and muted rumblings about secret suppers for certain mass circulation columnists were occasionally heard, Roosevelt appears to have attracted relatively little criticism on this score.

It is difficult to see why. Several favored journalists were given the privilege of direct access to the president. Arthur Krock, for one, scored some notable successes. In 1936, he floated a trial balloon for the president following a private conversation at Hyde Park, to which the journalist had been invited as an overnight guest. After Roosevelt had outlined his "grand design" for dissipating European tensions, a plan involving a meeting with the heads of the major states abroad, Krock, having secured an undertaking from Roosevelt not to repudiate the story, wrote a front-page report in the *New York Times* giving details of the scheme. Incensed at its publication, the other reporters urged Roosevelt to deny the story's authenticity. The president kept his undertaking to Krock to the extent of refusing to comment on the article but, according to Krock's account, encouraged Henry Wallace to tell the press that in his judgment the story had no foundation. Then came Krock's success of March 1937, when, in a cleverly phrased letter, he offered the president a chance to elaborate on the issues

surrounding his Supreme Court proposal. Apparently finding the proposal irresistible, Roosevelt granted the exclusive interview, agreed that
the article should appear on page one of the *Times*, and decided to
weather the press resentment that might follow—though, in the event,
its ferocity probably surprised him. The article won for Arthur Krock
the 1938 Pulitzer Prize and for Franklin Roosevelt the temporary
enmity of the Washington press. Roosevelt declared himself chastened
by the experience, but his promised reformation was short-lived: later
the same year another *Times* reporter, James Kieran, was granted an
exclusive interview which became the basis for an article on the manner
in which Roosevelt kept in touch with public opinion, which appeared
in the *Times* on 3 October.[22]

Much more significant, however, was the highly favored treatment
that journalist George Creel received at Roosevelt's hands. Unbe-
known, apparently, to the Washington press, Roosevelt repeatedly
used Creel's articles to outline his plans and purposes and to test public
reaction to them. It was surprising that Roosevelt, who, in this respect,
was behaving much as Hoover and Theodore Roosevelt had done, was
able to escape the notice of the correspondents and the odium which
such practices, had they been discovered, must have attracted, especially since every article was preceded by an editorial comment that
boasted of its authoritativeness "due to Mr. Creel's long and close
association with the President." Often Roosevelt actually dictated
whole paragraphs to Creel. In August 1935, while reporter and president were preparing the piece entitled "Looking Ahead with Roosevelt"
(the Supreme Court had ruled against the NRA in June) Roosevelt
dictated two long paragraphs which, so far as the Court was concerned,
signaled his broad thinking, if not his precise intention. "Fire that," he
observed grimly, "as an opening gun." Surprisingly, however, the
article was ignored by the rest of the press. In December 1936 Roosevelt
again, as he thought, tested the winds of public opinion. At his suggestion, he and Creel produced an article entitled "Roosevelt's Plans
and Purposes," which, when it was published in the 26 December issue
of *Collier's*, contained a three-column discussion of the Supreme
Court. Creel anticipated an explosion both in Congress and in the
press, but, he has recalled, "incredibly enough, not a newspaper in the

country caught the significance of the statement."[23] Roosevelt's under-estimation of the extent of the adverse reaction to his Court proposal may, in the light of such events, be less surprising.

Others who received favored treatment were Anne O'Hare Mc-Cormick, special columnist of the *New York Times*, whose efforts to obtain exclusive interviews were quite indefatigable, columnist Drew Pearson, and Joseph Alsop, Jr., who enjoyed the advantage of being related to the president's wife. In Pearson's case, Roosevelt occasionally provided him with information in areas of his special concern, such as the recognition of Russia, or with damaging material on members of the administration whose loyalty he distrusted.[24]

Nor could the official policy of impartiality be said to have embraced representatives of the Negro press, the record of whose attempts to obtain admission to Roosevelt's press conferences is protracted, tortuous, and eloquent.[25] Beginning in 1933, Negro journalists, whether as individuals or as members of Negro press organizations, began petitioning the White House for permission to attend Roosevelt's press conferences; but not until January 1944 was the color line finally broken. In the intervening period, Stephen Early turned aside repeated requests for representation either on the grounds that only reporters for daily newspapers were admitted (almost all Negro newspapers were weekly publications), or, whenever journalists from daily publications applied, by asserting that admission would automatically follow their accreditation by the House or Senate press galleries or the White House Correspondents' Association, to which bodies he suggested they apply. From this procedural labyrinth, however, no aspirant ever successfully emerged.

In fact, Early's assertion that only representatives of daily newspapers attended the president's conferences was disingenuous. Indeed, the loophole through which the Negro press finally stepped was the discovery by its representatives that twenty-five correspondents of weekly trade journals were attending Roosevelt's meetings with the press on a regular basis. Additionally, it lay well within the competence of Stephen Early to exercise discretion in favor of a newsman who did not meet the formal requirements for press conference admission, as he did, for example, in the case of Walter Winchell, an avid supporter of

the administration, whom Early arranged to have admitted as often as
Winchell desired. With the president's tacit approval, it is clear, the
policy of impartiality toward the press in the Roosevelt White House
operated within sharply defined racial limits.

In the most fundamental sense, the satisfactory relationship between
Franklin Roosevelt and the Washington press endured because it
rested on the solid bedrock of mutual advantage. The correspondents'
regular contacts with the president at his press conferences meant that
they were plugged in to an inexhaustible news source; that, under
congenial circumstances, they could ask their questions, check their
leads, and obtain the information on which their daily stories would be
based. Theirs, they knew, was a privileged position: they learned of
many important administration programs, of which Lend-Lease was
but one example, before Congress, and were in a unique position to
gain early insights into presidential thinking. Occasionally, Roosevelt
might reveal a basic attitude directly, as he did when a correspondent
asked after his Quarantine Speech whether there was any likelihood of
a conference of peace-loving nations and he replied: "No, conferences
are out of the window. You never get anywhere with a conference."[26]
But to reporters who knew Roosevelt well, and who had developed a
finely calibrated sensitivity toward him, a shift in nuance, a chance
remark, a facial expression, the manner, even, in which he dodged a
question, could convey meaning. Having absorbed his perspectives, the
Washington correspondents could often anticipate his policies.

It is significant that the possible advent of Dewey in 1944 quickly
revived the reporters' apprehensions. Dewey, a contributor to the 15
May 1944 issue of the *Guild Reporter* pointed out, did not like reporters, hated to be asked on-the-record questions, hated, equally, to
talk off the record on any subject. Dewey refused, moreover, to take
responsibility for his pronouncements, insisting, rather, that his remarks be attributed to "sources close to the Governor," a ploy which
Albany correspondents derisively referred to as his "insinnuendo technique." The Republican presidential aspirant, the writer continued,
favored exclusive interviews, obstinately declined to give out lists of
appointments and visitors, and had no relish for his conferences with
the press.[27] Against Franklin Roosevelt, none of these charges could

have been laid. After twelve years, he still stood supreme, his press conferences regarded by reporters as "the best show in Washington," exciting combinations of "real-life drama, history in the making and superb personal performance."[28] He was, as he always had been, a reporters' president, and, the correspondents continued to believe, likely to be superior in his dealings with the press to any of his rivals.

For Franklin Roosevelt, the advantages of his regular contacts with the Washington press were equally substantial. The very frequency of his press conferences ensured that big stories would break either in a conference or so close to one that the president could make an immediate comment, which helped to portray Roosevelt as the focus of national activity. So far as the business of government was concerned, he used his press conferences to communicate executive action and to address the country with more flexibility and regularity than he could in either formal message or fireside chat. The conferences became a springboard for the launching of ideas, an effective means of shaping public opinion. At them, he could explain to the correspondents, and, through them, to the people, the broad thinking behind an administration program, dramatizing ideas in a fashion that was likely to be reflected in headlines and news stories. One outstanding example of this technique was Roosevelt's discussion of Lend-Lease at a press conference the month before he introduced the bill incorporating that proposal; his widely publicized garden-hose analogy probably helped materially to explain to the public the manner in which he had decided to help Britain and to mobilize support for his scheme.[29] Further illustrations can be found in the press conferences which he held before his special messages on the devaluation of the dollar or reorganization of the Supreme Court. His annual prebudget press conferences with the correspondents—another Roosevelt innovation—served the same purposes.

In a wider political perspective, Roosevelt's press conferences were an integral part of a well-established sequence by which he sought to mobilize public opinion behind important policy initiatives. Initially, in a fireside chat, he would state the nature of a problem and outline the general principles which should govern its solution; there would follow meetings with the press at which, using background and "off-the-

record" discussion, he would thoroughly acquaint the reporters with
his thinking so that they could write knowledgeably (and sympathetically) about the policy; and finally, would come a message to Congress
recommending a specific piece of legislation to meet the problem at
hand.[30]

Moreover, the general run of press conference questions helped
Roosevelt to gauge public opinion, an advantage which he specifically
acknowledged. Martin Gumpert, after observing Roosevelt's reactions
to press conference questions, perceptively described the process:

> From the way questions are formulated, from the tone of the inter-
> viewers, he senses the mood of the country, the weight of current
> events, trends, problems—all coming to a head in these few minutes.

Understanding Roosevelt's mastery of that technique, and his pride in
that mastery, and in his ability to catch the drift of public thinking,
Gumpert shrewdly observed: "With Roosevelt, one has the feeling not
only that he regards the living contact with public opinion as a political
necessity, but that he enjoys it as an esthetic treat."[31]

Additionally, Franklin Roosevelt was able to use his press conferences
to influence the content of news and the manner of its presentation.
The "straight" reporting of press conference news, on which he always
insisted, actually favored him, for the dispatches relayed his background comments without suggesting that Roosevelt's views may have
been superficial, or inconsistent with those he had previously expressed. But beyond this, he used his personality with telling effect.
Franklin Roosevelt's charm and persuasiveness were legendary—columnist Mark Sullivan once said of him that he "could recite the Polish
alphabet and it would be accepted as an eloquent plea for disarma-
ment"[32]—and in his press conferences he exploited these assets powerfully to shape the correspondents' attitude toward the events which they
heard him discuss, so that many took their cues from him and adopted
his perspectives. Martin Gumpert wrote:

> With easy cadences, with tiny pauses, with the nuances of expression
> that flit across his mobile face, he exerts a compelling influence. . . .
> One can almost see the skill with which he turns situations to his own
> account, how he, in turn, by means of gestures and pauses, by

shadings of his temper, conducts the choir of the press with his invisible baton.[33]

Other procedures were more overt. Roosevelt might suggest that an editorial of which he approved be repeated by the rest of the press, or that the press initiate the discussion of a particular issue; he might bring remote pressure to bear on editors to follow closely a government handout ("I hope very much that the managing editors will read it [a statement on the Agricultural Adjustment Act]," he told a press conference on 25 October 1935, "because the average managing editor in the East knows no more about farming...than a chicken"); or he might simply try to write an article for the reporters ("In other words," he would frequently say, "here is the way I would put it if I were writing the story."). Roosevelt could negatively influence news content by using off-the-record comments to douse false rumors, or prevent the press from encroaching on sensitive areas, or even, as he did with Ramsay MacDonald's Consultative Pacts scheme at a press conference on 10 May 1933, virtually kill discussion of a subject, for a time, in the press.

Nor were journalistic standards neglected. Through his regular press conferences, Roosevelt was able to put continual and at times intense pressure on the correspondents to conform to those standards of reporting which he believed to be appropriate. Described by Arthur Krock as "the greatest reader and critic of newspapers who had ever been in the President's office," Roosevelt read eleven newspapers each day, scrutinizing them, publisher J. David Stern has revealed, with the aid of a photographic memory, received many press clippings through the mail and an extremely detailed weekly analysis of press reaction to his policies from the Division of Press Intelligence. Therefore, when the reporters assembled before him, he knew what many of them had written. His standards were exacting, his admonitions continuous, and the consequences of not measuring up to his somewhat arbitrary requirements often decidedly unpleasant. At his press conferences, Roosevelt might ridicule wayward reporters, or even attack them directly, analyzing an offending article line by line and branding various statements "deliberate lies." "Mr. Roosevelt," one correspondent ruefully observed, "could be as rough and tough as a Third Avenue blackjack artist."[34]

Unquestionably, also, Roosevelt determined to use his press conferences to create a supply of news which could, by dominating the front pages of the nation's press, overcome the heavy editorial opposition which he so often faced.

The policy was quite deliberate: Roosevelt remarked repeatedly that as long as the nation's press reported what he did and said, he cared little what editorial writers or columnists had to say. It was also highly successful. "For four years," noted columnist David Lawrence in June 1937, Roosevelt had "dominated the best pages in the American newspapers...." He "was on page one more often than was any opposition influence or factor. He got page two almost as frequently." Lawrence went on to invite his readers to look back over the issues of any daily newspaper covering Roosevelt's first term. They would find, he asserted, that Roosevelt had been constantly in the headlines, a circumstance which Lawrence attributed to the president's unique ability to create news stories.[35]

Actual research has provided some confirmation of Lawrence's estimate. A total of ninety-two Roosevelt press conferences during the period 1 November 1934 and 31 October 1935 produced one hundred and four page-one stories in the *New York Times*, twenty-one of which were considered of sufficient importance to rate two- or three-column headlines. A selection of seven White House press conferences in the three-month period preceding the 1936 presidential election produced six front-page reports in the *New York Times*, six in the *Baltimore Sun*, six in the *New York Herald Tribune*, and four in the *Washington Post*; sixteen White House press conferences in the three-month period prior to the 1940 election gave rise to thirteen page-one stories in the *New York Times*, thirteen in the *Washington Post*, twelve in the *New York Sun*, eleven in the *Baltimore Sun*, eleven in the *Washington Times Herald*, nine in the *New York Herald Tribune*, and eight in the *New York World Telegram*.[36]

Roosevelt's ability to dominate the front pages was recognized by others as well as Lawrence. Reviewing press treatment of the president in the 1932, 1936, and 1940 elections, *Editor and Publisher*, in its 12 December 1942 edition, commented that Roosevelt had owned the page one of the nation's newspapers day after day, and that his ideas had

had to be placed before the public whether editors agreed with him or not. Asked who was the best columnist in America one editor replied: "That's easy—Franklin Roosevelt. He can hit the front page with a column of his own opinions any day he wants to. And we've got to print it."[37]

In the senses explained, therefore, the Washington correspondents' need to obtain news was at least matched by Franklin Roosevelt's need to create it. Their relationship was complementary; their dependence mutual. For over twelve years, Franklin Roosevelt and the Washington press were, in journalist Walter Davenport's words, "united in holy newslock."[38]

I Can Appreciate What You Are Told to Write

It would not merely be perverse to point out, in opposition to Franklin Roosevelt's public account of his relations with the press, that he often quarreled with the reporters whom in practice he liked and sometimes cooperated with the columnists whom in principle he detested. His attitude toward the latter was openly contemptuous: in his 1938 statement he dismissed them; in his White House press conferences he continually derided and mocked them. The output of columnists was, Franklin Roosevelt believed, based on speculation or gossip, molded to suit the requirements of their clients, and unworthy of serious attention by their readers or professional respect of their colleagues. Columnists themselves, he inferred, were absurdly pretentious, attempting a task which he himself had found to be impossible, and presuming, on the basis of knowledge that was clearly inadequate, regularly and authoritatively to comment on weighty national affairs. Their views were narrow, their judgment feeble or corrupt, and, by fostering the unfortunate demand for interpretative stories, they insidiously weakened the press itself, causing the reporters to emulate their method but the public to deride its results.

Many of the nation's columnists, it is clear, Roosevelt had reason enough to resent: their widely circulated attacks on him were often vituperative and abusive; their criticism of his administration unrelenting. Among those who opposed the president, Frank Kent, Westbrook Pegler, Paul Mallon, David Lawrence, Mark Sullivan, Hugh Johnson, and Walter Lippmann were the most significant. Kent, whose column "The Great Game of Politics" was syndicated nationally in 1934, and was, by 1938, appearing in 112 newspapers with an estimated

mated total circulation of seven million,[1] supported Roosevelt initially, but, progressively alienated by New Deal reforms, became, by the end of the president's first term, one of his bitterest opponents. From that time, he raked the New Deal with fierce and unvarying criticism.[2] More vitriolic than Kent was Westbrook Pegler, whose column, quaintly titled "Fair Enough," was syndicated nationally in 1933, and, by 1938, was featured in 110 newspapers with an estimated total circulation of 5,907,389. Described by a fellow journalist as "one of the most consistently resentful men in the country" (a friend named a stretch of water at Pegler's country home "Lake Malice," and his small boat *Rancors Aweigh*), Pegler attacked the president with such dedication that a contemporary was moved to observe that "there have been very few offenses of the sort that can be laid to public officials—libelous or non-libelous—which Pegler hasn't charged against Roosevelt."[3] Also predominantly hostile to the New Deal were Paul Mallon, whose column, by 1938, appeared in 200 newspapers, with a massive total circulation of twenty-five million, David Lawrence, whose daily commentary was carried by 133 newspapers with an estimated circulation of six million, and that rambunctious New Deal refugee General Hugh S. Johnson, whose daily outpouring was featured in 67 newspapers with an estimated circulation of four million. Referring to the general's journalistic style, fellow columnist Westbrook Pegler observed that Johnson was "like Dempsey," for "once that bell rings, he knows nothing but punch, punch until something drops."[4] Many of the general's punches were aimed at the president.

More staid and more cerebral, if no less determined in his opposition, was Mark Sullivan, whose daily column was carried by 54 newspapers with an estimated circulation of four million. This highly respected conservative journalist wrote with an urbanity and literary grace which, notwithstanding his disagreement with Sullivan's opinions, sometimes earned the president's appreciation. At his press conference on 21 August 1942, Roosevelt read one of Sullivan's more felicitous pieces into the transcript, with the specific purpose of ensuring its inclusion in any history of the times which might be written— a request which it would seem churlish now to ignore. Prompted by a remark by a presidential visitor that he had "no worthwhile comment" for the reporters, Sullivan had suggested that, if the visitor had "no copyright on those few short words. . .they could be advantageously used by some other Washington officials who face press conferences." Sullivan continued:

> If all officials were as immune as the impassive Mr. Patterson from feeling that courtesy or other motive requires them to satisfy the newsmen with something interesting or amusing—in that event the quantity of words that go out of Washington would become at once diminished—(Laughter)—and more informative. (More laughter)

Roosevelt called the piece "one of the grandest things I have ever read."

Also temperate in tone, although generally critical or neutral in his attitude toward Roosevelt and the New Deal, was Walter Lippmann, whose column appeared, by 1938, in 160 newspapers with an estimated total circulation of over eight million. An early supporter of the president, Lippmann took specific issue with him in 1935 over legislation to control holding companies and the "soak the rich" tax program. More generally, the columnist took neither a strongly positive nor negative position toward individual New Deal measures, but, having expressed initial, if qualified agreement, characteristically moved to a position of increasing opposition. On the other hand, Lippmann frequently sent messages of congratulations to the president and had several private meetings with him.[5]

Unquestionably, though, the daily output of such writers constituted formidable press opposition to Franklin Roosevelt and his policies.

However, Roosevelt was not, among mass circulation columnists, without support. Walter Winchell, a frequent presidential visitor, was unquestionably Roosevelt's most ardent journalistic admirer. Writing effervescently to the new president in December 1933, Winchell observed:

> Busy as you are, sir, I realize you haven't time to tune in on your New York correspondent—me.
> However, I want you to know—how often I have mentioned you in an affectionate way on the radio and in my newspaper column, which is syndicated throughout the country.

The column to which he referred was carried, in 1939, by 150 news-papers, with an estimated total circulation of 8,570,000. By October 1941, Winchell's enthusiasm had not diminished: in a telephone mes-sage to the White House he expressed the desire to give Roosevelt "a great big hug" for what he was doing for the country.[6] Another avowedly pro-New Deal columnist was Jay Franklin, whose daily com-ments appeared, by 1939, in 30 newspapers with an estimated total circulation of 4,140,000. From 1941, this columnist supplied Roosevelt with intelligence gathered by an agency based in New York, set up with direct assistance from the White House. By these means, a vast quan-tity of memoranda, covering subjects ranging from labor unrest at home to estimates of the holdings of strategic materials by foreign countries, and including, also, statements on attitudes within the busi-ness community and estimates of public opinion on various subjects, was forwarded to the president.[7] Equally dedicated, though less numer-ically significant support for Roosevelt, was provided by Samuel Graf-ton, whose column "I'd Rather Be Right," appeared in the *New York Post* in 1939, and was later distributed by the Bell Syndicate.

Although there was some ambiguity in the relationship between Drew Pearson and Robert S. Allen and Roosevelt, both columnists aligned themselves, broadly, with the New Deal. Their "Merry-Go-Round" column, carried by over 600 newspapers with a total circula-tion of above 20 million was, a contemporary noted, "regarded as a kind of White House pet and sniffed at accordingly in many circles." The close alliance between Pearson and Harold Ickes was widely rec-ognized; but from Roosevelt, too, Pearson sometimes obtained val-uable inside information. For his part, Allen offered the president sympathetic political advice. Thus, for instance, having returned from a political survey of the Midwest in October 1940, Allen wrote to Roosevelt expressing alarm at his prospects in that area, urging him to hammer away at the idea that he was for peace, and advising him to visit Illinois and Indiana.[8]

The list of columnists who, in some significant measure, supported or cooperated with Franklin Roosevelt can be extended. Ernest Lind-ley, the president's biographer and friend, wrote sympathetically of his policies in a column which, by 1938, appeared in 35 newspapers with a total circulation of 4,500,000. Though his propensity occasionally to offer sharp criticism of the administration was recognized, on the whole, Lindley's admiration for the New Deal proved durable. The oracular and very formidable Dorothy Thompson, too, was a powerful, if rather belated, addition to the Roosevelt camp. Originally a critic of the New Deal, she swung her support behind Roosevelt in 1940, fought enthusiastically for him in the campaign of that year, and submitted material for use by his speech writers. Her column, which first appeared in the *New York Herald Tribune* in 1935, was, by 1938, syndicated nationally in 140 newspapers with an estimated circulation of 7,500,000.[9] The writings of Joseph Alsop and Robert Kintner, also, were generally supportive of New Deal objectives. Alsop was concerned to rebut the charge that he and Kintner were New Deal insiders, whose writings reflected administration policies, but the plausibility of his denials is not increased by correspondence between the two columnists and members of the administration. In May 1939, for instance, Kintner assured Henry Morgenthau, who was under fire from reporters over the origins of articles which Alsop and Kintner had written for the *Saturday Evening Post*, that neither journalist had revealed the fact that Morgenthau had assisted them, and had denied that suggestion when it had been put to them by the reporters.[10] Though essentially nonpartisan, Raymond Clapper, whose column was, by 1938, carried by 49 newspapers with an estimated circulation of 3,653,395, was another who probably supported New Deal measures as often as he criticized them.[11]

Sufficient evidence can be found to show, therefore, that, while Franklin Roosevelt may have continually had to suffer the barbs of many of the nation's mass circulation columnists, he also received, from others of the same group, a not insignificant measure of support. As he himself explained, however, his implacable opposition to newspaper columnists was quite uninfluenced by his relations with them as individuals, or the favorable treatment which he sometimes received at their hands. That was made plain, if ever it needed to be, a few months before Roosevelt's death. Following his description of columnists as "an unnecessary excrescence on our civilization," Lowell Mellett, until recently a member of the administration, but at the time of his writing a columnist for the *Washington Evening Star*, enjoined the president to "quit saying unkind things about us columnists," and, reminding Roosevelt that he was not without support among that group, enclosed some favorable columns by Jack Bailey to illustrate his point. Roosevelt, however, was unrelenting. A columnist's political orientation, he explained to Mellett, was immaterial; and, so far as their attacks were concerned, he, himself, was "waterproof." Even were all columnists to support him, he would feel precisely the same.[12] Roosevelt's objection, he made plain, was not merely to columnists who opposed him, but to columnists per se, and derived from his appreciation of their insidious influence on journalism as a whole, and from his appreciation of the threat which they posed to his own role and to that of the press within the democratic system.

With the other major aspect of Franklin Roosevelt's account of his relations with the working press, on the other hand, there could be less disposition to quarrel. The statement which he made in 1938 that "the great majority of newspaper correspondents who cover the White House are personally friendly to the Administration," though tendentious, to a degree, in its easy equation of their attachment to him personally with their support for the New Deal politically, was nevertheless valid as a generalization when he made it, and would have been broadly appropriate as a description of reportorial attitudes had he chosen, subsequently, to repeat it. But what survives as a generalization must yet be subjected to important qualifications; a comprehensive study of the relations between Franklin Roosevelt and the Washington press reveals that the correspondents' allegiance to the president survived in spite of basic disagreements and periodic disputes which were neither small in degree nor unimportant in nature or ultimate significance. Of such conflict, Roosevelt's own account of his relations with the press gives no hint.

Some conflict was inherent, built into a situation in which both president and press sought to be the first to reveal government plans and policies—the president in order that he might make his own stage-managed announcements, at the most politically opportune time; the reporters in order that the press could fulfill its assumed function of keeping the public informed in advance of governmental thinking, so that political debate could not be circumscribed, nor government action precipitate.[13] Their search for such advance knowledge led newsmen to cultivate various members of the administration who, under guarantee of anonymity, supplied information helpful to their own schemes or aspirations and frequently damaging to those of their rivals. Some "leaks" were unintentional, as when Arthur Krock tricked Secretary Woodin into revealing that the United States was about to abandon the gold standard;[14] most were deliberate and politically or personally inspired. Examples abound. Raymond Clapper, for one, was made privy to cabinet discussions through conversations with, at various times, Attorney General Robert Jackson, Navy Secretary Knox, and Commerce Secretary Jesse Jones. In December 1941, Harold Ickes revealed to Clapper the contents of a letter, which he had sent to Roosevelt, complaining about the president's decision to give Henry Wallace and the Economic Defense Board control over oil shipments and supplies, suggesting to Clapper that the decision was in conflict with a previous order conferring such powers on himself, and protesting that he had not been consulted about the change. At the same time he charged that Harry Hopkins was the cause of most of his troubles and revealed that Jones had failed miserably in his efforts to build up stockpiles of rubber, much to the president's dismay. Secretary Ickes, it is well known, confided also in Drew Pearson, and Arthur Krock's connections within the administration were extensive and, from a newsman's point of view, lucrative.[15]

Roosevelt made strenuous efforts to control the release of unauthorized information: his own abundant news output, together with the deluge of official publicity emanating from the vast army of New Deal press agents, dulled the reporters' appetites for news of factionalism and damaging feuds; he sought to funnel all information and contacts with the press through departmental press agents; and he lectured departmental heads on the dangers of discussing with reporters matters relating to other departments or agencies. On a personal level, the president gathered information on the social activities of members of the administration, even down to the lower echelons, especially on their relations with newsmen, and then brought pressure to bear on his subordinates to sever such contacts in order to eliminate the journalists' sources of information.[16]

Roosevelt's efforts met with considerable success: "In no recent time," wrote Turner Catledge in the *New York Times* of 29 December 1936, "has the door been shut so tightly against information other than that passed out officially." But if the flow of inside information could be reduced, it could not be eliminated, and in Roosevelt's press conferences, his anger over its release continued to surface.

A second fundamental conflict arose, Arthur Krock asserted, out of a difference in essential obligation between government and press. In deciding whether to publish information, a newspaper had merely to ask whether it was true, whether it had been legitimately acquired, and whether it ought to be public property. Information might meet all of these criteria, Krock pointed out, and yet be regarded by a president as diplomatically premature or politically confusing. This difference in essential obligation generally lay behind presidential denials of news stories which were substantially true, a practice in which Roosevelt not infrequently indulged and from which this correspondent occasionally suffered. Thus, on one occasion, Roosevelt denounced Krock, accused him of damaging the standing of the nation, and complained to the reporter's employer, because the journalist made public information which, by Krock's account, had been given to him by the secretary of state. Krock had a similar experience in 1938. Shortly after the Czechoslovakian crisis of that year Jesse Forrestal and Paul Shields, two presidential associates, told the reporter of an attempt by Roosevelt to arrange a meeting with Hitler for the purpose of trying to avoid war. Three weeks later "another very important person in Roosevelt's unofficial group of advisers" confirmed the story, adding that Roosevelt had sent an emissary to attempt to arrange the meeting and assuring Krock that there were no restrictions on publication. Believing that the story would be good publicity for the president, Krock wrote it. Roosevelt responded by denying its authenticity in a statement which read: "I have read the Krock story in the New York Times. It is not true, but otherwise it is interesting and well written." On this occasion, the reason for the denial seemed more capricious. Asked subsequently, by Attorney General Frank Murphy, why he had repudiated a story so favorable to himself, Roosevelt's reply, as recounted by Murphy to Krock, was, "He had his timing wrong. It didn't happen when he said it did. It happened three months before." [17]

At a more prosaic level, Roosevelt's desire for occasional privacy clashed with the need which the press association reporters, in particular, recognized to cover his activities at all times. On his wartime trips Roosevelt called these wire-service men "ghouls," or sometimes "vultures," and complained that they were merely waiting for something to happen to him. Their rejoinder was that they waited *in case* anything should happen, and that the public had a right to know, at all times, what the president was doing and where he was. An exasperated Roosevelt once remarked that the reporters and photographers would never be satisfied until they followed him to the toilet.[18]

Leo Rosten, who conducted extensive interviews and questionnaires with the Washington correspondents toward the end of Roosevelt's third term, dated the first serious dissatisfaction with Roosevelt among the reporters from the early part of 1935. As the New Deal began to falter, so too, in some cases, did the reporters' allegiance to it. They looked for its intended benefits without finding them and began to suspect the long-term suitability of what they now saw to be a piecemeal emergency program. A series of uncharacteristically inept acts by the president widened the breach. In February 1935, he told a press conference that he would not support state NRA legislation, but, when Governor McNutt of Indiana protested, he extricated himself from a difficult situation by charging the pressmen who had reported his remarks with "misrepresentation." Similarly, his "horse and buggy" strictures against the Supreme Court, following its verdict against the NRA, offended many journalists and weakened their faith in his political sagacity, just as his denial that he had recommended so called "soak the rich" legislation after spokesmen for the administration had announced that he had, amazed and angered them. There was keen disappointment, too, when Roosevelt cut off a persistent questioner by telling him: "This isn't a cross-examination," for the reporters had come to feel that this was their right.

Other complaints were more personal and, in Rosten's estimation, more trivial. Roosevelt's resort to humor to evade press conference questions was resented, his smile, facial expressions, and use of first names were suspected. There was a growing feeling, too, against "off-the-record" remarks, which were seen, increasingly, as a means of protecting the president, rather than helping the reporters.

The correspondents' adverse reaction to some of the president's traits, Rosten surmised, was accentuated by a sense of their own professional shortcomings. They, who liked to think of themselves as hard-boiled cynics, incapable of being taken in by smooth words and clever political techniques, had succumbed, they now saw, to Franklin Roosevelt's charm and to the deluge of New Deal publicity. Seduced by that charm and ballyhoo and handicapped by their own keenly felt inability to produce anything better than an impressionistic and surface interpretation of events, they had created, and themselves believed in, the Roosevelt myth—the notion that Franklin Roosevelt was, by a long way, the shrewdest and most artful politician ever to occupy the White House. That myth having been dispelled, the correspondents' sense of professional guilt gave a sharper edge to their growing disenchantment with the president.[19]

As their continuing commentary on his performance makes plain, beneath the apparently calm surface of Roosevelt's relations with the Washington correspondents, such criticisms continued as an undercurrent. Even those reporters who thought highly of Roosevelt occasionally found his cordiality forced and irksome. Some, on the outer fringe of his press conferences, began to resist their premature termination by front-row colleagues who they believed had fallen under the spell of Roosevelt's charm. Roosevelt's evasive techniques also caused irritation. Drawing attention to the president's habit of evading questions with jokes or quips, one reporter noted that a growing number of serious correspondents were declining to laugh unless they were genuinely amused. Moreover, although Roosevelt was almost invariably a good news source, that did not imply, such was his dominance of his press conferences, that the correspondents could obtain from him the information which they sought; week after week some might be forced to go away without answers to questions which they considered to be of pressing national or local importance. Declared newsman James L. Wright:

Mr. Roosevelt is a man with the air of candor, but lacking in candor. He adroitly sidesteps and dodges. Unless one is hypnotized by being called by his first name, and will trade a presidential smile for a piece of news, he must admit that is so.[20]

The tone of other comments was more bitter. Newsman Eugene Kelly described the press conferences as "in the main, colossal jokes. . . nothing but concentrated sales talks for the New Deal." Off-the-record comments might have the effect of "swelling the collective chests of newcomers, who labor under the delusion that they have been singled out from the rest of mankind as repositories of highly confidential information," but were, in reality, "only another ruse of the New Dealers," who realized that prefacing their remarks by such a phrase would doubly ensure their publication.[21]

Not only was there, among the reporters, suspicion of the president's charm, irritation at his evasiveness, resentment against his domination, and distaste for his propaganda, but, once the turbulence of the early emergency had settled, the whole apparatus of New Deal publicity began to take on a more menacing appearance. Government publicity was freely acknowledged never to have been so effectively organized or widely disseminated: there were skilled press agents in every department or agency, and, in large organizations such as the NRA or AAA, publicity divisions comparable in scale with those possessed by a large newspaper; the handouts which these bodies issued were plentiful (the NRA alone distributed more than 5,200 by July 1934), and often better written than if the correspondents had prepared them themselves. At first, official New Deal publicity evoked, if not open enthusiasm, grudging acceptance. But, as the immediate economic emergency passed, criticism came to be directed at the size of the official publicity machine, its voracious appetite for staff, and a disturbing tendency to make press agents the sole contact between the press and the administration. By March 1935, one correspondent was remarking acidly that reporters now seldom wrote their own stories but had become mere messenger boys running between the government bureaus and their own offices carrying statements prepared by press agents. "Any boob," he observed with feeling, "can deduce, a priori, what type of 'news' is contained in this rubbish. Sprinkled with the saccharine juice that drips from the press agent's pen, the handouts exude a supreme confidence in the worthiness of the Administration and its leaders."[22]

The complicated field of press ethics and reportorial standards was a subject on which, though in no sense an expert, Franklin Roosevelt nevertheless dogmatized, never tiring of giving the Washington reporters advice, criticizing their dispatches, lecturing them about their accuracy, and making confident pronouncements as to the standing of the press in American society. "Never in my 20 years here [in Washington]," declared Raymond Clapper in November 1939, "have newspaper reporters received as much advice as to how to do their work, and as much warning against light-fingered handling of important news situations."[23] What many reporters were reluctant to accept, however, was Franklin Roosevelt's fitness to offer such gratuitous advice. To Arthur Krock, for instance, it was remarkable that a man whose sole experience in the collection and presentation of news had been as a reporter on the Harvard *Crimson* should give the impression that his knowledge of such matters was superior to that of lifetime professionals.[24]

The Washington press corps was, after all, an elite journalistic group, whose educational standard, occupational record, level of remuneration, and prestige were conspicuously above the average for their occupation. Leo Rosten, whose 1936 sample of 127 Washington correspondents included representatives of 186 leading dailies, all the press associations, and leading columnists, found that 72.4 percent of the group had attended college, and that 51.1 percent of these had graduated; that special correspondents questioned had worked for their present newspapers an average of 12.5 years, and press association reporters for an average of 11.3 years; that the average years of newspaper work for the group was 18.8, and their average period of employment in Washington 9.7. Rosten discovered, also, that, for the majority (75.5 percent), journalism had been a deliberate career choice, and that, throughout the newspaper industry, few editorial positions carried greater prestige than that enjoyed by the Washington reporters.[25] Such a competent, dedicated, and professionally self-conscious group were not always willing to accept with passivity and equanimity lectures on their professional shortcomings by a man whose credentials as a press expert they suspected, whose conception of their role seemed unrealistically circumscribed, and whose depiction of their motives was often, in their view, grotesque.

Out of Franklin Roosevelt's attempts to police press standards came the bitterest conflicts between him and the Washington press. At a press conference on 9 August 1937, Roosevelt, singling out from several similar stories a report by Ernest Lindley on the visit of Edward Flynn to Hyde Park and the possible connection between that visit and the New York mayoralty campaign, commenced to read the article line by line to the reporters, making clear, at each stage, his objections to it. The transcript is instructive:

The President [reading from the article]: "Hyde Park, N.Y., August 8—Edward J. Flynn, Democratic leader of the Bronx and of the Roosevelt wing of the Democratic organization in New York City, conferred with President Roosevelt here today."
Lie number one, he did not "confer."
"Neither the President nor Mr. Flynn would say anything about their talk."
This is a statement and it is a lie. You never asked me. "In fact, some effort was made to keep Mr. Flynn's presence here a secret."
The effort was made by bringing him down in my car to a place you were all going to be. That was the effort. That was a lie just as was the U.P. story [to which Roosevelt had previously referred]. The same holds true, it just is not true, Ernest.
Q (Mr. Lindley): Mr. President—
The President: So far we have had three of them.
Q (Mr. Lindley): Would you like to give me a chance to reply?
The President: Let me read some more. Let us see if there is anything else in it. "But as to Mr. Flynn's purpose, there was no occasion for doubt. As in the 1933 Mayoralty campaign, he is again seeking the intercession of the national administration on behalf of the Roosevelt section of the Democratic set-up in New York city in a campaign against Mayor F. H. LaGuardia."
If that is based on anything that happened yesterday, it is a lie and, obviously, it does refer to what happened yesterday.

In the exchanges that followed, Lindley, though not without argument, admitted that his statements that Roosevelt and Flynn had "conferred" and that neither would make any comment on their "talks" were misleading and gave the president legitimate ground for complaint. But the issues of the purpose of Flynn's visit and of whether or to what extent an effort had been made to conceal his presence were not, in the reporters' minds, as clear-cut. Since Roosevelt had told them only that some of his neighbors were coming to Hyde Park for a social visit, and Presidential Secretary McIntyre, in charge of appointments, had informed them that only one person of political significance (John March) would be attending, the correspondents had been surprised by Flynn's appearance and intrigued by an overt reference to New York city politics which he had made. In attacking the correspondents, Roosevelt, in effect, argued that, had Flynn been invited for political reasons, he (Roosevelt) would have informed the reporters of that fact. As he had not done so, Flynn ought merely to have been regarded by them as a "neighbor" who had come to Hyde Park for a "social visit," his acknowledged importance as a political figure notwithstanding. And, the president reiterated, in furious and unreasonable hyperbole, "I still insist if I want to see God Almighty socially, it is social news and not political news."

Not inconceivably, an ingrained skepticism as to the unvarying veracity of politicians may have contributed to the reporters' reluctance to accept the official interpretation of the events surrounding Flynn's visit, but, in any event, in subsequent exchanges their position hardened. Lindley, in particular, refused to accept that the inaccuracies in his own account had resulted from the pressures under which he worked or that that account was entirely fanciful. "I know your difficulties," Roosevelt said to him. "You have to turn out so much stuff a day." "I am under no compulsion to write news for my paper," the reporter replied stiffly, "...the fact remains that Mr. Flynn is a factor in New York city politics and his visit to you is a matter of extreme news interest." What followed was vintage Roosevelt:

> I understand. You fellows are placed in such a position very often.... We can talk about it in the family and off the record. I can appreciate what you are told to write...it does not take away, in any way, from my affection for the group of you.... That is why the newspapers are losing the influence they had ten years ago...because of interpretative stories that do not hold water.

Another rancorous exchange between the president and the reporters followed publicity given to the idea that America's frontier in Europe in its battle against fascism was the Rhine, a suggestion that Roosevelt was reported as having made to the Military Affairs Committee of the Senate. Asked, at his press conference on 3 February 1939, for a clarifying statement on foreign policy, Roosevelt launched into a blistering assault on the correspondents. Some members of the Senate and many newspaper owners, he charged, were deliberately misrepresenting the facts to the American people. Angrily pointing to several newspapers on the desk before him, he complained that there was not one story or headline in any of them that did not give a false impression. The upshot of such reporting was that the American people were beginning to realize that what they were reading in the press was "pure bunk." Asked specifically whether he had, as reported, told members of the conference that the Rhine was America's frontier in democracy's battle against fascism, Roosevelt branded the story a deliberate lie. The reporters' subsequent questions revealed their resentment and incredulity.

Outside the conference those correspondents whose integrity had been impugned sought out their informants in an effort to have their stories confirmed, and, before long, Roosevelt's account of the meeting was being sharply challenged from Capitol Hill. *New York Times* bureau chief Arthur Krock found the president's behavior disingenuous. An expert on "leaks," Roosevelt could have prevented their occurrence on this occasion by issuing a joint communique at the conclusion of his meeting with the senators. Not only had he not done this, but, Krock pointed out, he had allowed the reports of the meeting to go unchallenged for two days before opening his attack on the reporters. What had prompted that attack, Krock surmised, was not protests in Rome and Berlin, but the strongly adverse reaction within the United States, which made it clear that two of Roosevelt's policy aims—the repeal of the Neutrality Laws and the defeat of the Ludlow war-referendum—had been hindered rather than helped by the story. But whatever its proximate cause, James Butler wrote in *Editor and Publisher* of 11 February 1939, the episode represented the correspondents' "first wide-open break with the White House."

The elite Washington reporters were not merely affronted by such major assaults: Roosevelt's dogmatic views on press ethics, his gratuitous advice on reportorial standards, his derisory remarks about their financial acumen, the manner in which he publicly ridiculed their most respected colleagues, the continual stream of insults which he directed against columnists, and his repeated assertions that the Washington correspondents were journalistic stooges who wrote what they were told—all these caused a predictable amount of irritation and resentment. "That he [Roosevelt] can still command the loyalty of the correspondents after such mortal affronts to their pride and stoutly defended integrity is," declared newsman Walter Davenport, "among the more remarkable of his accomplishments."[26]

The onset of war brought new tensions. In the months following Pearl Harbor Roosevelt placed new, and, to the correspondents, unnecessary restrictions on their coverage of his movements, refusing to allow reporters to board his train or even to publicize his periodic trips to Hyde Park. Protest, especially by the three press associations, which, between them, supplied news to every newspaper in the country, was incessant, but, for a time, futile. The first major concession came in September 1942, when the three White House wire-service reporters were permitted to accompany Roosevelt on a two-week tour of the nation's defense plants. But, even here, the president's refusal to allow them to file their stories until the tour had ended produced what, to the correspondents, was an absurd situation in which Roosevelt was seen by thousands across the country on a trip which the American press was forbidden to report. The situation seemed, moreover, to afford the president some enjoyment: he drove through Seattle, waving cheerfully to thousands—"an entire city off the record," a reporter laconically remarked—and jokingly told a huge audience to forget that they had seen him as his trip was supposed to be secret. The crowd of 20,000 was amused; the reporters were not.[27]

Simmering resentment boiled over when Roosevelt returned to Washington. In a letter of protest signed by thirty-five correspondents, the signatories complained that they had been unable to obtain any satisfactory explanation as to why the president's security had required complete suppression of all news about his tour until after its completion. The atmosphere at the press conference that followed was tense, and when Roosevelt observed that there was less understanding of the requirements of war in Washington than elsewhere, and that his view was based on a more intimate knowledge of the country than the reporters possessed, he was bluntly reminded by one of them: "That isn't our fault."[28]

The correspondents were incensed, too, at the lack of consideration shown to them during Roosevelt's wartime meetings with other heads of state. Particularly contemptuous, in their eyes, was their treatment during Roosevelt's first meeting with Churchill, at which the Atlantic Charter was signed. They reacted with extreme skepticism to an official announcement that the president, coincidentally with an exodus of top military personnel from Washington, was undertaking a fishing trip, and with mounting anger to a situation in which the *Potomac*, which he was supposedly aboard, remained off the coast of Swampscott, Massachusetts, monotonously and provocatively beaming to them a daily bulletin: "The day was clear and beautiful and the party enjoyed good fishing." Though Roosevelt held a brief meeting with American reporters following his return from his Argentia rendezvous with Churchill, most of their information about the conference filtered through from the British press, two of whose representatives, in breach of an agreement with Roosevelt, had been surreptitiously included in Churchill's official party. Columnist Paul Mallon spoke for the Washington corps when he complained that the American press had "certainly got a shabby deal, if not a double-crossing, in a great event of American history." [29]

The Washington press was further antagonized by the president's treatment of its members at his overseas conferences. At Cairo, accredited correspondents were kept from the conference by barbed wire, and, after the conferees had moved to Tehran, the reporters were held at Cairo under military orders. Once again, the British made the American press look foolish, breaking an agreement, as they had done at the Atlantic Charter meeting, by releasing a communique on the Cairo conference prematurely, and keeping their own citizens informed about the conference by quoting "world travelers" as they arrived in Portugal. Not until Yalta did Roosevelt include representatives of the American press as members of his official party, though he did, for the Casablanca conference, to even the account with Churchill, arrange to have George Durno, a captain in the Air Transport Corps but previously INS correspondent at the White House, added to his party as a baggage officer. [30]

Within the United States, correspondents protested angrily against the severe restrictions placed on the reporting of the United Nations

Food Conference at Hot Springs in 1943. Asked, by a disgruntled correspondent at his press conference on 18 May, about reports that restrictions on press coverage of the conference had threatened the freedom of the press, Roosevelt attempted to deflect the question by suggesting that the reporters might also like to have a tier of benches in the Cabinet Room and in his office. "What's wrong with that?" quipped an obliging reporter, and, in the manner of so many others, a difficult situation was avoided.

By and large, the voluntary censorship system worked effectively from its inception after American entry into the war, but at times, to the Washington press, its administration appeared petty, its restrictions ludicrous. Behind its protective shield, Arthur Krock complained, even presidential subordinates took grateful refuge, and correspondents were prevented, in the interests of national security, from reporting such mundane events as the weekend visits of Henry Morgenthau to his farm. Roosevelt's cavalier abuse of the voluntary system caused special resentment. During the 1944 campaign, newsmen pointed out, the president had traveled openly through various cities and made speeches to unselected audiences, without questions of security having been raised. He had also welcomed reporters aboard his train and lifted practically every restriction on the reporting of his movements. But, the minute he had been reelected, the censorship door had been slammed shut once again. In February 1945, Director of Censorship Byron Price bluntly warned Stephen Early that Roosevelt's obduracy in restricting press coverage of matters of little security concern was threatening the entire voluntary censorship system.[31]

Under the stress of war, Roosevelt occasionally impugned not only the reporters' integrity, but also their patriotism. On 24 March 1942, he informed a press conference that there would be no successful fifth column in the country were it not for the "sixth columnists" who were a vehicle by which such propaganda could be distributed. Asked to elaborate, he declined, on the ground that he would have to include many of those who were listening to him. In December the following year, he astonished the Washington press by presenting an Iron Cross to reporter John O'Donnell, an action which, the reporters quickly realized, had the effect of smearing O'Donnell with a pro-Nazi brush on the eve of the trial of a suit which he had brought against pro-New Deal publisher J. David Stern and the *Philadelphia Record* over an editorial which described him, among other things, as a Naziphile and an anti-Semite. Commenting on Roosevelt's action, the strongly anti-New Deal *Washington Times Herald* described it on 31 January 1943 as "a new low in his campaign of vilification against those correspondents who have incurred his displeasure"; but even the generally sympathetic Charles Hurd wrote of a general consensus among newsmen that Roosevelt had hit below the belt.[32]

Franklin Roosevelt's injunction, so frequently repeated, that the Washington reporters should maintain a clear distinction between "straight" news, which concerned itself with "the facts," and "interpretative" writing, which embellished such reporting with speculation, analysis, or other extraneous comment, was asserted with dogmatism, defended with resolution, and applied with inconsistency. Columnists and editorial writers, both of whom were interpreters rather than reporters, he could afford to dismiss: he heaped insults on the former, and, though he could not deny the latter their function, he was fortified by the belief that their efforts at interpretation, when they were not misguided or malicious, were puerile and derisory in comparison with his own. With the Washington reporters, on the other hand, whose ostensible concern was with "the facts," Roosevelt saw a continuing danger that "straight" news reporting could become sullied by "interpretation," and it was against this tendency, and the loss of public confidence in the press which it would cause, that he repeatedly warned. "It must be hell to have to interpret," he told reporters at a press conference at Hyde Park on 7 November 1934, implying, characteristically, that they were being forced by their employers to do it. "But you know, that is one reason why...the American public today are paying less and less attention to news stories because so many of them have become interpretative." "Give them [the people] the facts," he declared, "and nothing else."

Among the professionals of the Washington press corps, however, the president's constant strictures against interpretation produced mystification. To many, the distinction which he drew between "fact" and "interpretation" seemed spurious, his pronouncements curiously inconsistent with his own press conference practice. If reporting was, as Roosevelt maintained, the retailing of facts as announced by the administration, such handling of news would amount to little more than the dissemination of propaganda. In any event, hard-and-fast distinctions were, they evidently believed, impossible to sustain: "Following this conversation," *New York Times* reporter Charles Hurd observed dryly, adding a skeptical postscript to his account of a discussion between Roosevelt and the reporters of the difference between fact and interpretation, "the correspondents carried out their work for that day by interpreting the President's reaction to the [congressional] election results." Nor, in the Washington reporters' view, did Roosevelt's injunction to "give them the facts and nothing else" sit happily alongside his suggestions that "If I were writing this story, here is how I would write it"; for, as Arthur Krock pointed out, when Roosevelt made such overt suggestions, the reporters were aware, even if he were not, that he was slanting information to suit his own purposes.[33]

But if Franklin Roosevelt's strictures against interpretation caused mystification or irritation among the Washington press corps, his assertion that its members were in journalistic bondage to the newspaper owners, whose antiadministration bias they were forced to reflect, provoked open resentment. Even in the press conferences, where argument was difficult, the president found himself, on this point, openly challenged. Again and again the newsmen denied Roosevelt's charge, but the fact that he continued to make it is significant, for it indicates that, while his very considerable antagonism toward the American press was usually vented on the Washington correspondents, its major object was the newspaper owners.

Three

The Group More Resented by the President than Any Other Group in American Life

If Franklin Roosevelt regarded the Washington reporters customarily with tempered affection and columnists invariably with lofty contempt, he reserved for American newspaper owners a more active and implacable hostility. In his 1938 statement he had drawn attention to their antagonism toward his administration and to what he believed to be their practice of requiring their reporter-employees to reflect that opposition in news dispatches; through his press conference comments and personal correspondence he developed a more elaborate critique. Newspaper publishers, he believed, were unfitted by background or training for their task, lacked journalistic talent, and had little grasp of their wider public responsibilities. In political outlook they were reactionary, in economic crisis obstructive, in war often unpatriotic, and, so firm was their commitment to "the counting room" rather than "the news desk," that they were incapable of editing newspapers "in the cause of democracy," and endangered "from within" the very press freedom about which they so tirelessly but fraudulently expressed their concern.

Owners, to Franklin Roosevelt, were the repository of press sins and shortcomings, to whom all responsibility could ultimately be attributed. Editors, no less than reporters, were firmly under their control: "It is not the editors," he told the reporters at a press conference on 26 August 1938; "Hell, most of the editors have got families. They cannot lose their jobs. They have to write what the owner tells them to." By implication, therefore, if the overwhelming majority of the press opposed the president, the owners were to blame; if its tactics were often deplorable, the owners were to blame; if support was lukewarm where it should have been enthusiastic, with carping criticism being substituted for active, two-fisted support, or the press debased its standards, or forfeited public confidence in its integrity, or initiated fear, or contributed to recession, the responsibility lay with the owners and publishers of America. "Lack of [public] confidence [in the press] today," Roosevelt told his annual conference with journalism teachers in December 1935, in a statement which illustrated the general set of his thinking, "is...because of the colored news stories and the failure on the part of some papers to print the news.... It is not the man at the desk in most cases. It is not the reporter. It goes back to the owner of the paper."

The depth of Roosevelt's antagonism toward publishers can be seen in the acerbity of his comments about them and the frequency of his criticisms. Sometimes he assailed particular foes, as when he wrote of Colonel Robert McCormick and Cissy and Joe Patterson that they "deserve[d] neither hate nor praise—only pity for their unbalanced mentalities."[1] More usually, however, he concentrated his hostility on owners as a group, and, in his press conferences, his attacks on them became a commonplace: "Almost every week," noted a *Kiplinger Washington Letter* of June 1937, "there's some White House 'crack' against newspaper publishers as a class—off the record and unpublished." Indeed, such was the frequency of Roosevelt's attacks that publishers were called the president's "favorite whipping boys," and, by columnists Joseph Alsop and Robert Kintner, "the group more resented by the President than any other in American life."[2]

Roosevelt's critique of American newspaper publishers and their activities serves occasionally to illuminate, but more usually to obscure, the pattern of his relations with several of the more important members of that group and the measure of opposition or support which, individually and collectively, they provided for his policies.

Even with William Randolph Hearst, who was eventually to attack the New Deal with sustained ferocity and with journalistic tactics which many besides the president would find distasteful, a long period of bitter opposition was preceded by a briefer period of harmonious personal relations and enthusiastic journalistic support. Hearst had played an important part in securing the nomination of Roosevelt, and, in the period between Roosevelt's election and assumption of office, discussed with him policies by which recovery could be achieved and the personnel of which the new administration was to be composed. The publisher produced an eleven-point plan for the former, and some gratuitous advice on the latter, opposing Al Smith and Owen Young, but supporting the inclusion of Baruch, Glass, Norris, and "a woman" as secretary of labor.

The Hearst press, which had campaigned for Roosevelt's election, greeted his inauguration and the decisive action of his first weeks in office with enthusiasm. Although his delight in the new administration was not unalloyed, the area of agreement between Hearst and Roosevelt was wide and when the president torpedoed the London Economic Conference in June 1933, the publisher's newspaper chain called the action "a modern declaration of independence." On a personal level, Hearst wrote to inform Roosevelt that he had been "doing a little work...telling the business people how fine you are," and surmised that, at the president's next election "we will make it unanimous."[3]

The 1934 general strike in San Francisco, for which the publisher blamed the NRA, weakened Hearst's attachment to the New Deal, and the tone of criticism in his newspapers sharpened. Nevertheless in May and again in October, the publisher was a guest at the White House.

The break came in 1935. In his annual message of that year, Roosevelt called on Americans to "forswear that conception of the acquisition of wealth which, through excessive profits, creates undue private power over private affairs and...public affairs"; shortly afterward, Hearst ordered his newspapers to open fire on the administration. Alarmed by the resulting volley of criticism, the president invited Hearst Editor-in-Chief Coblentz to the White House for discussions; but the brief truce which followed ended abruptly on 19 June when Roosevelt asked Congress for heavier taxes on the wealthy. "The President's message," an outraged Hearst wrote to his chief editors, "is essentially Communism."[4]

The allegiance of Colonel Robert McCormick to the New Deal was of shorter duration. The publisher of the *Chicago Tribune*, who had known Roosevelt from their school days at Groton, supported him in 1932, and, for a time, maintained his enthusiasm for the new president. In May 1933, he invited Roosevelt and his wife to stay at his home when they came to Chicago to open the World's Fair. "It seems to me," McCormick wrote, "you are making very good weather of it in the storm." Roosevelt, who had to decline the invitation, responded with a suggestion that McCormick visit him in Washington.

In these early months of the new administration, McCormick was impressed by Roosevelt's decisive action and ability to implement his policies, but by the autumn of 1933 his enthusiasm had begun to wane. At a speech in October, McCormick, as chairman of the American Newspaper Publishers' Association Committee on Freedom of the Press, expressed his disquiet over attempts being made to bring the press under the provisions of the National Industry Recovery Act, but when, at a subsequent press conference on 27 October, a *Tribune* correspondent asked about a disposition to curb the freedom of the press, Roosevelt, recognizing the source of the question, advised the reporter to "tell Bert McCormick he is seeing things under the bed."[5]

From that time the personal antipathy between Roosevelt and Mc-Cormick grew, and the *Tribune* maintained toward the New Deal a virulent and raucous opposition.

The opposition of Henry Luce, owner of *Time, Life,* and *Fortune*, to the New Deal was more subtle, his relationship with Roosevelt less clear-cut. Visiting Roosevelt soon after his inauguration, the publisher had been captivated by the new incumbent, and, for a period, his enthusiasm was reflected in his publications. However, *Time* was offended by the recognition of Russia in November 1933, and its attitude toward the administration became more critical. In the economic sphere, although *Fortune*, Luce's business magazine, gave generally sympathetic coverage to the first year of the New Deal, there was an undercurrent of concern in both that publication and *Time* about New Deal extravagance and its constraints on business.

Following Roosevelt's success in the midterm elections, he was named *Time*'s Man of the Year, but the magazine boosted Landon in 1936, generally continued its criticism of Roosevelt during his second term, backed Willkie (with whom Luce was closely associated) in 1940, and supported Dewey in 1944.[6]

Against this prevailing background of opposition by Luce's publications to the Roosevelt administration, the relations between Luce and Roosevelt never were close and sometimes were hostile.[7] There were occasional meetings between the two, one of them, in May 1939, being prompted by a "perfectly wonderful tribute" which Luce had paid to Roosevelt in a recent speech. Otherwise, Roosevelt's communications with the publisher were almost exclusively concerned with objections by the president to the content of the latter's publications and of their style, which, in a reference to *Time* magazine, he once called "a serious detriment to the future of successful democracy in the United States." Denunciation of that magazine was never more dramatically accomplished than in November 1941, when the president publicly attacked *Time* over an article on the political crisis facing the Popular Front government of Chile. "While the Popular Front swayed," *Time* had informed its readers, "bushy mustached President Aguirre . . . spent more and more time with the red wine he cultivates." Aguirre died shortly after this report, greatly compounding the American government's embarrassment. At a press conference Roosevelt announced that the government had been forced to apologize for *Time*'s disgusting lie, and that it had been informed by its ambassador in Chile that the article had made a significant contribution to Nazi propaganda against America.

Roosevelt's broadside was followed by a tenuous rapprochement: in the full flush of patriotic enthusiasm after the attack on Pearl Harbor, Luce wrote:

> The drubbing you handed out to *Time* before December 7 was as tough a wallop as I ever had to take. If it will help you win the war I can take worse ones. Go to it! and God bless you.

In his reply Roosevelt praised the publisher's letter for its patriotism and sportsmanship, citing it as an example of the spirit of national unity which would ensure military success. "The waters of Pearl Harbor," he wrote, "have closed over many differences which formerly bulked big."

Franklin Roosevelt's relations with other publishers were more durable. By comparison with his cousin, Colonel Robert McCormick, with whose journalistic orientation he was eventually to become so

closely identified, Captain Joseph Patterson maintained a friendship
with Roosevelt and an allegiance to his administrations which were to
extend into the president's third term.[8] It was Patterson, whose ac-
quaintance with Roosevelt dated from their school days, who, in the
early months of the new administration, launched the movement to
provide the new incumbent with a swimming pool. From the outset,
too, Patterson's mass circulation *New York Daily News* fought strongly
for the New Deal, its editorial of 6 March 1933 constituting a virtual
journalistic blank check:

> This newspaper now pledges itself to support the policies of Presi-
> dent Franklin D. Roosevelt for a period of at least one year from
> today; longer, if circumstances warrant. . . . Whatever Mr. Roosevelt
> may urge as methods of attacking these emergencies, we expect to
> support him, to withhold constructive criticism, to give the new
> leader a chance.

In the event, the *News'* allegiance was to continue for almost eight
years.

Relations between Patterson and Roosevelt during the president's
first two terms were close and cordial: there were consultations between
them at the White House and at Hyde Park, affectionate messages,
and requests by the publisher for advice. A letter sent by the president
to the publisher in November 1936 was illustrative: after thanking
Patterson for his "very splendid" support during the campaign, Roosevelt estimated that the *News* had won more votes in New York City than
had all the political meetings and speeches put together.

Yet by 1940 Patterson's views were changing in a manner which
would bring him and Roosevelt into direct and violent conflict. On his
return from a European trip in 1939, Patterson wrote a series of
articles containing strikingly inaccurate assessments of the character of
the Nazi regime and the likelihood of war. When Hitler invaded Poland
a month later, the *News* urged loyalty to the government, but its
isolationist orientation was becoming more marked. Having supported
Roosevelt as the man who was keeping the United States out of
"Europe's war," the *News* broke with him over Lend-Lease, and, by
October 1941, was declaring that the conflict should now be named
after the president, since it had been he who had involved the United
States in it.[9]

A temporary reconciliation was effected, following the Japanese attack on Pearl Habor, when Patterson called on Roosevelt in order to confess that his isolationist policies had been misconceived. In a sustained attack, during which he read to Patterson a series of *News* editorials critical of the administration, the president reduced the publisher to tears. But Patterson's change of heart was short lived, and the *News* quickly settled down to a policy of strident opposition, which continued for as long as Roosevelt was president. It was probably alone among important dailies in not carrying an obituary editorial on the first possible occasion after Roosevelt's death.[10]

The at times significant discrepancy between Roosevelt's critique of newspaper owners as a class and his association with individual members of that group emerges more clearly from a consideration of his relations with Roy Wilson Howard.[11] In many ways Howard was a publisher after the president's own heart, having graduated to that position after a long and successful career in journalism, which culminated in his appointment as general news manager, and later president, of the United Press. In 1922 Howard became a partner and the dominating influence in the Scripps newspaper group, and by the mid 1930s was the head of a press empire that embraced a long chain of daily newspapers, the United Press, and the Newspaper Enterprise Association feature syndicate.

His initial doubts about Roosevelt having been resolved at a meeting between himself, Scripps-Howard Editor-in-Chief George B. Parker, and Roosevelt in early October 1932, Howard threw the very considerable weight of more than forty Scripps-Howard newspapers behind Roosevelt in the campaign of that year, and, throughout the president's first term, the publisher's support for the New Deal was wholehearted. "Don't let the fact that I was not enthusiastic about Frank Roosevelt before his nomination confuse you as to my present state of mind," Howard wrote to Stephen Early on 6 March 1933. "I had all my enthusiasm for Hoover *before* his election. My enthusiasm for Roosevelt has developed steadily since his nomination." In the same letter Howard promised full cooperation and invited suggestions from the White House as to the ideas which his newspapers ought to propagate. He also forwarded to Roosevelt a copy of a dispatch, which he had prepared for Scripps-Howard editors, directing them to praise Roosevelt's recent statements and the administration's actions in editorials and news reports. Obviously gratified, the president thanked Howard for his "fine message." Anxious further to demonstrate his support, the publisher brought to Roosevelt's attention a reply which he had made to a letter from Parry D. Saylor, president of the Canada Dry Corporation, in which Saylor had suggested that the corporation's advertising in Howard's newspapers was not unrelated to their editorial attitudes toward the New Deal, and implied that an increase in the volume of the former would follow a more critical orientation in the latter. Howard's loyally pro-administration response must have disappointed Saylor, but ought to have pleased the president. "I am so sold on the efforts he [Roosevelt] has made," he wrote, "that neither as an editor nor as an individual am I disposed to indulge in any back-seat driving at the present time." The aim of Scripps-Howard newspapers would be to continue to support the president in his efforts to "construct a sounder and a more progressive social and economic structure."

Howard's continuing enthusiasm for Roosevelt was reflected, editorially, in his newspapers. On 15 April 1935, an editorial in the *New York World Telegram* urged the president's opponents to "Stop the Calamity Howling!" The country's fate, Howard's newspaper declared, was "almost completely in the hands of Franklin Roosevelt." Should any political enemy "tie his hands," the economic lives of the American people would be imperiled. The editorial went on to invite the president to state what popular support he desired and to identify "the men or the interests who are blocking...recovery." He would not, the *World Telegram* added threateningly, "be disappointed with the results." The response of Roosevelt, to whom Howard sent a copy of the editorial, was effusive. When, on 23 May 1935, the *World Telegram* saluted the president for his veto message on the bonus, Howard again forwarded a copy of the editorial to Roosevelt, adding, on this occasion, his own tribute: "Your speech yesterday scored a new high in my opinion. It was just *great*." It was small wonder that Stephen Early wrote to Roosevelt that the Scripps-Howard newspapers were "truly carrying the flag for the New Deal."

The relationship between Howard and Roosevelt remained close throughout Roosevelt's first term. The publisher was a frequent presidential visitor, and wrote repeatedly to offer advice or sympathetic criticism, or to pledge his continuing support. In May 1935, Howard warned Roosevelt that an attempt was being made to suggest that he would be unperturbed if Congress overrode his proposed veto of the Patman soldiers' bonus bill. Adopting the publisher's suggestion, Roosevelt clarified his position in a personal statement to a press conference. A speech which Roosevelt delivered in April 1936 evoked, from Howard, a characteristically enthusiastic response. He had, he said, been elated by Roosevelt's words. The speech was "a generation ahead of most of the political yammering eye [sic] have heard during the past eight months." Roosevelt responded with an invitation to Howard to stay overnight at the White House. Howard continued, too, to seek Roosevelt's advice as to the editorial policies which his newspapers ought to adopt. His request, toward the end of Roosevelt's first term, for "fresh information and guidance" led to another conference with the president at the White House. Following it, Howard again pledged his newspaper chain's wholehearted cooperation: "We are," he told Roosevelt, "going to give you—or honestly *attempt* to give you—a full 100% of our support."

Howard's efforts to cooperate with Roosevelt went beyond his editorial endorsement of New Deal policies. The celebrated and supposedly spontaneous exchange of letters between the president and the publisher in September 1935, over the need of business for a "breathing spell" following a hectic period of New Deal reform, was a contrived and carefully orchestrated move in which Roosevelt and Howard collaborated closely in an attempt to allay the fears of business on the one hand and to permit the president to make a full public statement in defense of the New Deal on the other. Following a meeting between himself, Roosevelt and Early in July 1935, Howard sent a draft of his "breathing spell" letter to the White House with a request that Roosevelt amend it in any way he wished and include in it any matter on which he desired to make public comment. "I believe," he wrote to Stephen Early, "[that] the stunt can be handled in a fashion to do some real good." Having substantially modified Howard's draft, Roosevelt had it released by the White House, together with his own slashing reply.

Beginning in 1937 editorial comment by the Scripps-Howard news-papers on the New Deal began to evince a more critical tone; but Howard continued to affirm his commitment to what he considered to be the essence of Roosevelt's program. In a telegram dispatched in July 1937, the publisher drew the president's attention to "the strongest and most unselfseeking newspaper support the fundamentals of the New Deal have today."

Relations between Roosevelt and Howard were strained by two inci-dents which occurred in 1937. On 4 October, the *New York Post* carried a report by Robert S. Allen of a speech made by the president at the opening of a flood control and irrigation project at Fort Peck, North Dakota. "The highlight of the President's speech," Allen wrote, "was a caustic spanking of Roy W. Howard." Although Roosevelt had not mentioned the publisher by name, he had, according to Allen's account, made scornful reference to a New York owner of newspapers, a "doubting Thomas," who, in a recent conversation with him, had urged that power and flood control projects be abandoned and the resulting jobless put on the dole, since one half of his own income was being taken by federal income taxation. Clearly perturbed, Howard wrote to Stephen Early seeking an explanation; but the press sec-retary's evasive response could hardly have reassured him. A short time later Howard questioned Early over a report that Roosevelt, at a press conference, had related substantially the same story about the un-named New York publisher, and, on being asked whether the publisher referred to earned a reputation for wearing "loud" ties, had replied: "You have it!" When Howard accepted a subsequent invitation to meet the president, he told Secretary McIntyre that the proposed conversa-tion might be "the beginning of various other talks or the end of all of them."

In the event, however, the conflict between Roosevelt and Howard was temporarily smoothed over. The meeting was followed by an off-the-record conference between the president and the editorial board of Scripps-Howard, and, shortly afterward, Howard sent Roosevelt an editorial by the chain's editor-in-chief praising the president's more realistic approach to the recession and his attempts to end the feud between business and government.

Although the deterioration in relations between Roosevelt and Howard continued, the point of complete rupture was never reached. In April 1939, the president arranged a meeting with the publisher after the latter's return from a European trip. A month later, Roosevelt wrote to Howard objecting to certain statements in a Scripps-Howard editorial, but, although his criticism was sharp, his letter ended on a note of friendship, which Howard, in his reply, echoed. However, when Roosevelt, in July 1939, criticized both Howard and the United Press directly over a report that he and Cordell Hull had disagreed over the language of a neutrality message, which the president planned to send to Congress, the publisher responded with less equanimity. Pointing out that both the story and the confirmations of it had come from highly placed members of the administration, Howard rebuked Roosevelt for using "the enormous power of your position to castigate working newspapermen whose good faith, loyalty and patriotism is...no more open to question than is yours or mine," and reproached him for overlooking, by his criticism, the fact that the Scripps-Howard newspapers had "editorialized and fought to the limit of our ability to support your stand and your program, on the neutrality and arms embargo."

The year 1940 marked the nadir in relations between Howard and Roosevelt. In June the president was angered by the refusal of Howard to undertake a survey of conditions in Latin America for the administration. The incident had an unfortunate sequel when, in September, Hugh G. Grant, American minister to Thailand, reported that, during a visit to the legation, Howard had bitterly attacked Roosevelt, accusing him of bad faith over the offer of the South American assignment, suggesting that he was mentally and physically exhausted, and charging that he was attempting to lead the United States into war. Informed of Grant's charges, Howard described them to the president as "an unconscionable perversion of the word and the spirit of the conversation."

The onset of war effected a measure of reconciliation. Writing, in April 1942, to inform Stephen Early, and, through him, the president, that he had recovered from a recent illness, Howard spoke glowingly of the efforts Roosevelt was making to boost public morale. Early's assurance that Roosevelt had been "delighted" at the news of Howard's recovery and "naturally pleased with your comments on the efforts he is making to win the war," did not quite capture the spirit of the president's blunt memorandum to his press secretary: "Action speaks louder than words." Encouraged by Early's response and oblivious of the president's, Howard wrote again almost immediately to pledge his full cooperation, and, shortly afterward, passed on to Presidential Assistant Lowell Mellett some comments made to a United Press reporter on the effectiveness of Allied propaganda in Europe, and an assessment by Jim Miller, South American manager of the United Press, of the political situation in Brazil, Argentina, Chile, and Uruguay.[12]

The closeness, over several critical years, of the relationship between Franklin Roosevelt and Roy Howard; the publisher's not inconsiderable enthusiasm for New Deal policies; the resulting support of the powerful Scripps-Howard press, wholehearted during Roosevelt's first term, persisting well into his second, and reviving after the outbreak of war—all these are obscured by the blanket criticisms which the president made of the newspaper publishers of America.

With the publishers of the *New York Times*, too, Roosevelt enjoyed, on the surface at least, extremely cordial relations.[13] His friendship with Adolph Ochs predated Roosevelt's election and continued until Ochs's death in April 1935. In an affectionate letter to the publisher in November 1933, Roosevelt expressed sympathy with Ochs over his recent illness and invited him and his wife to stay overnight at the White House. "Do not," he wrote in conclusion, "consider this a command, but only the request of an old friend of yours who greatly likes to see you."

Roosevelt's relations with Ochs's successor, Arthur Hays Sulzberger, were marked by periodic meetings between them, the occasional affectionate exchange of greetings, efforts by the publisher to cooperate with the war effort, and attempts by the president to discipline the *Times* when it strayed from the path of journalistic rectitude. At the suggestion of Henry Morgenthau (who sent word, through Presidential Secretary Watson, that "he [Morgenthau] had a very good reason for suggesting that you [Roosevelt] ask Arthur Salzberger [*sic*] and his wife up here while you are at Hyde Park," and that Roosevelt "would understand"), Sulzberger had a discussion with Roosevelt at Hyde Park in October 1937, and the two met with some regularity following the outbreak of war. In January, 1940, Sulzberger sent to Roosevelt a dispatch from the *Times'* Berlin correspondent giving details of the Reich's ban on news, and, in October of the following year, with obvious patriotic pride, a collection of the wartime editorials of the *Times*. On his return from an overseas trip late in 1944, Sulzberger wrote: "I am overcome with wonder at what we are doing in the Pacific war...and only hope I can find the way to reflect some of that feeling in the columns of the New York Times."

Under Ochs and Sulzberger, the *Times* backed Roosevelt in 1932 and 1936, switched to Willkie in 1940, largely because of its opposition to the third term, but returned, albeit belatedly, to Roosevelt in 1944. On crucial issues between elections, the newspaper supported the president more often than it opposed him.[14]

By Roosevelt's standards, Eugene Meyer, the banker who bought the *Washington Post*, had come from "the counting room" rather than "the news desk," but, again, the president's own dealings with this publisher were marked by friendliness rather than hostility, and, particularly after the outbreak of war, by offers from Meyer of assistance and indications of support.[15]

Beginning in 1938, the publisher supplied the president with the results of opinion polls which had been commissioned by the *Post*. Thus, for example, in March 1941, Meyer called Roosevelt's attention to the results of a series of polls which showed that the transfer of destroyers to the Allies would be approved by 56 percent of the population and opposed by 26 percent, that there was sharp public hostility to strikes in defense industries and overwhelming support for projected federal moves to deal with them, and that men of draft age favored the Lend-Lease Bill. Meyer also sought appointments with Roosevelt after his return from overseas trips, in 1939 and 1941, for the purpose of passing on information likely to be of value, and sent the president messages of congratulations after his wartime speeches.

Under Meyer, the *Post* applauded the early New Deal initiatives, swung against Roosevelt in 1935, and maintained a generally critical attitude toward his domestic policies from that time, but gave strong support to the administration's foreign and defense policies. On critical issues throughout his presidency, the newspaper supported Roosevelt more often than it opposed him.[16]

The list of publishers with whom Franklin Roosevelt enjoyed cordial relations can be extended. His friendship with William Allen White, owner and publisher of the *Emporia Gazette*, preceded his presidency, endured throughout it, and easily transcended any dislike which Roosevelt may have had for newspaper owners as a class. A lengthy and affectionate correspondence between the two reveals its strength.[17] There was more than a little justice, too, in Roosevelt's claim, made at a press conference on 15 April 1937, that White, a Republican and the owner of a Republican newspaper, "agrees with me three years and a half out of every four"; messages of appreciation from the president for supportive editorials written by White were not infrequent. This note of nonpartisan cooperation was struck, also, in June 1938, after Roosevelt had asked White for a confidential assessment of one of the candidates for the Republican primaries in Kansas, whom Roosevelt had heard was "openly a fascist and...showing KKK tendencies." In response to Roosevelt's pledge to keep the source of the information confidential, White wrote:

> If John Hamilton puts me up against the wall and Jim Farley stands you up beside me, each of us for trafficking with the enemy, I hope someone will lend us a flag so that we can hold it up and tell the world that we died for our country and to hell with the party.

Later, in his capacity as chairman of the Committee to Defend America by Aiding the Allies, White was to serve as an intermediary between Roosevelt and Willkie in an effort to prevent the issue of the administration's foreign policy from dominating the 1940 presidential campaign.

On other occasions, White wrote to the president with entreaties, or to offer encouragement or advice, while, for his part, Roosevelt sought the counsel of White on pressing international problems. In December 1939, for example, Roosevelt made a direct request to White to come to the White House. "I need," said he, "a few helpful thoughts from the philosopher of Emporia." Pointing out in his letter that the world

situation was growing progressively worse, Roosevelt discussed the
dangers to the United States inherent in the Russo-German non-
aggression pact, and expressed his general fear that the serious implications of developments in Europe were being greatly underestimated
by the American public. "Therefore, my sage old friend," he concluded, in a tone which catches the spirit of the relationship between
the two men, "my problem is to get the American people to think of
conceivable consequences without scaring the American people into
thinking that they are going to be dragged into this war. Think it over
and do come down to Washington soon."

Although his relationship with Roosevelt was not as close as was
White's, the basic allegiance to the New Deal of J. David Stern was
never in doubt. When Stern, owner and publisher of the *Camden* (New
Jersey) *Courier*, the *Philadelphia Record*, and, from 1933 to 1939, the
New York Post, first met Roosevelt before the 1932 Democratic Convention, he was "completely disarmed by his charm," and, having been
convinced by Roosevelt and Samuel Rosenman that Roosevelt had
accomplished 90 percent of his program as governor of New York,
decided to support his bid for the presidency.

Almost immediately Stern was involved in a scheme, devised by
Roosevelt, to brand Al Smith as the favorite of big business at the 1932
convention. Having seen the political possibilities in a situation in
which Frank Hague, Smith's campaign manager, had sought the
assistance of General Atterbury, Republican national committeeman
and president of the Pennsylvania Railroad, in his attempt to woo
Philadelphia Democratic leader John O'Donnell into Smith's camp,
Roosevelt asked Stern to feature the story in the *Philadelphia Record*
and to send five thousand copies of the newspaper to James Farley at
Chicago. "I see a headline," Roosevelt mused: "Triple Play Hague to
Atterbury to O'Donnell." Stern himself handled the story, which, he
was later to recall, "worked like a charm." [18]

Halfway through Roosevelt's first term, Stern became concerned
about what he regarded as "the President's trend toward the right." In
a letter to Senator Joseph Guffey, in February 1935, he complained
that Roosevelt was appearing to favor big business, and that he, Stern,
had not seen the president for over five months, which seemed to

indicate that Roosevelt was "avoiding outspoken liberals." Reaffirming his faith in the president's sincerity, he nevertheless expressed a desire to discuss with him the real purposes of the administration. The overture brought a quick response from Roosevelt, to whom, naturally, Stern's letter was forwarded: "Read this," he instructed Secretary McIntyre, "and send for Dave Stern."[19]

The alliance between Roosevelt and Stern was demonstrated clearly in the O'Donnell case. On 29 January 1943, John O'Donnell, head of the Washington bureau of the *New York Daily News*, was awarded $50,000 damages in a libel suit against Stern and the *Philadelphia Record*. The origin of the suit was a story written by O'Donnell in April 1941, which asserted that American warships were convoying Lend-Lease supplies to Britain. When Stephen Early denounced the story as a "deliberate lie," the *Record* used the phrase as the title of a front-page editorial, written by Stern, which accused O'Donnell, among other things, of pro-nazism and anti-Semitism. According to the violently anti-New Deal *Washington Times Herald*, which discussed the trial on 31 January 1943, "not for one minute...did counsel for the paper,...relax its efforts to persuade the jury that President Roosevelt was personally interested in the outcome of the case in behalf of his old friend, J. David Stern." The newspaper which was being sued, noted the *Times Herald*, "has stood high in New Deal favor for consistent support of the Administration and its aims." It was on the eve of this trial that Roosevelt had presented O'Donnell with an Iron Cross, and just prior to that episode, the *Times Herald* reported, Stern had visited the White House.

Franklin Roosevelt enjoyed the support of Stern's publications for the entire period of his presidency. Those newspapers attacked publishers who opposed the Newspaper Code, and relentlessly assailed the Hearst press, in particular, for its opposition to the New Deal. When a *Fortune* survey in May 1938, revealed that Roosevelt's popularity remained high—54.7 percent of the people supporting him as against 34.4 percent who did not—the *Post* analyzed New York newspapers in order to demonstrate that the city's readers had been kept in ignorance of this significant information. In a private conversation with Stern after the 1944 election, Roosevelt expressed the view that the support of

the *Courier Post* had been decisive in New Jersey, and that the useful-
ness of the *Record* had transcended the boundaries of its city and
state.[20]

Another avowedly pro-New Deal publisher from whom Roosevelt
received constant support was Marshall Field, owner of the New York
newspaper *PM*, and of the *Chicago Sun*. The former publication, an
experimental newspaper which accepted no advertising and was controlled by its own staff, caused great interest amongst journalists when
it was launched in 1940, and, from the outset, gave enthusiastic backing to Roosevelt's administration. A month after it had begun, the
newspaper's Washington correspondent delivered to the president a
series of pro-administration editorials written by its editor, Ralph
Ingersoll, together with a message from Ingersoll that *PM* was to be
"150% for Roosevelt."[21] Nor was the pro-New Deal orientation of
Field's *Chicago Sun*, launched in 1941 as a rival to McCormick's
Tribune, ever open to question: from the outset this publication gave
vociferous backing to the president's policies and attacked his enemies.
Of it, William Randolph Hearst wrote, in the 21 November 1942
issue of *Editor and Publisher:* "The President of the United States
wanted a new deal morning paper in Chicago, a political and personal organ. Mr. Marshall Field, III . . . arranged to give the President
his desire." Significantly, it was as the result of a complaint by Field
that the Roosevelt administration brought its antimonopoly charge
against the Associated Press. In March 1942, five months before
Assistant Attorney General Arnold filed the suit against the Associated
Press, Field had a lengthy discussion with the president about his
complaint.[22]

In the light of his generally hostile attitude toward them as a group,
the nature of Franklin Roosevelt's relations with some of the more
important newspaper publishers of the United States is surprising and
the substantial measure of support which they provided for his administration somewhat unexpected. So far as McCormick, and even
Hearst, both of whom were later to oppose him with such ferocity, are
concerned, it is not remarkable that Roosevelt, in his resentment
against them, should have overlooked their early support; nor could the
president's relations with Henry Luce have been expected to modify any

antagonism toward publishers which he may have felt. But, as one moves across the spectrum of publishers, past Howard, who cooperated closely with the president into his second term, and Patterson, who supported him until his third, and looks more closely at the cordiality of his relations with Ochs, Sulzberger, and Meyer, and the strength of his friendship with White, and considers, further, the enthusiastic backing which he received from Stern and Field, so does the gap between the rhetoric of Roosevelt's public statements about publishers and the reality of presidential-publisher relations widen, and the discrepancy between his antagonism toward publishers as a group and his fruitful relations with some publishers as individuals become more marked. There is a further consideration. Even on the basis of the amount of publisher and press support which Roosevelt is now seen to have received, the president's repeated assertions that he faced overwhelming press opposition begin to look suspect. For if Franklin Roosevelt exaggerated the opposition of newspaper publishers, might he not also have exaggerated the degree of opposition which he faced from the press as a whole, since, at least by his own argument, the latter was very much a function of the former?

Four

The Famous Eighty-five Percent

Objective assessment of Franklin Roosevelt's frequently repeated assertion that he was opposed by the overwhelming majority of the nation's press—mockingly referred to by him as "the famous eighty-five per cent"[1]—is feasible, particularly if attention is confined to the treatment of his administration in the daily newspapers of America. For such an assessment, an examination of the declared political affiliations of the nation's daily newspapers, as collected annually by *Editor and Publisher*, the leading trade journal of the newspaper industry, is an appropriate starting point.

Responses to a questionnaire sent by *Editor and Publisher* to newspaper publishers late in 1935 indicated that, of 1,800 daily newspapers for which statistics were collected, 316 or 17.56 percent were claimed by their publishers to be Republican, 328 or 18.22 percent to be Democratic, 211 or 11.72 percent to be Independent-Republican, 153 or 8.50 percent to be Independent-Democratic, and 792 or 44.00 percent to be Independent in their political affiliation. What is notable here, besides the fact that the proportion of Independent newspapers was relatively large—more than twice as great, in fact, as the number of Democratic or Republican newspapers—is that the number of Democratic newspapers slightly exceeded the number of Republican newspapers, and that the combined total of Republican and Independent-Republican newspapers was only slightly greater than the combined total of Democratic and Independent-Democratic publications. Five years later the distribution of political-affiliation was virtually unchanged, with 292 or 15.62 percent of the nation's dailies declaring themselves to be Republican, 301 or 16.16 percent to be Democratic, 209 or 11.22 percent to be

Independent-Republican, 233 or 11.87 percent to be Independent-Democratic, and 838 or 44.98 percent claiming to be Independent.[2]

It is unnecessary to postulate anything more than a very rough correlation between political affiliation and editorial policy in order to appreciate that an assertion that 85 percent of the nation's press opposed the president collides immediately with these figures, since, for such a claim to have been true, it would be necessary to envisage a situation in which, on the most likely assumptions, not merely all Republican, Independent-Republican, and the very large number of Independent daily newspapers in the United States opposed the president, but that, in addition, all Independent-Democratic and something over one in ten of the Democratic newspapers did so as well.

Nor is the charge of 85 percent press opposition borne out by statistics collected by *Editor and Publisher* on the political alignment of the nation's daily newpapers during presidential election campaigns. Even in the crucial campaign of 1940, when press opposition to the president reached a crescendo, a survey by *Editor and Publisher* of two-thirds of the nation's English-language dailies revealed that 289 or 22.71 percent of the newspapers which responded were supporting Roosevelt, that 813 or 63.86 percent were supporting his opponent, and that 171 or 13.43 percent were not committed to either candidate. Such figures certainly revealed solid press opposition to Roosevelt, but, even here, the estimated percentage of the nation's press that opposed him in his controversial third-term bid was 64, not 85. In earlier presidential elections it was considerably less: in 1932, Roosevelt had received the backing of an estimated 40.52 percent of the nation's daily press, as against 52.02 for Hoover, with 9.45 percent being uncommitted; in 1936 the corresponding figure for Roosevelt had been 36.1 percent, as against 57.10 percent for Landon, with 5.8 percent uncommitted. A later poll, conducted just prior to the 1944 election, found that Dewey was receiving support from 61.10 percent of the daily press, that Roosevelt was favored by 22.00 percent, and that 17.90 percent of dailies were uncommitted.[3]

Even during presidential election campaigns, therefore, when newspaper opposition to the New Deal was at its height, the actual percentage of newspapers which openly declared their opposition to it did not approach the figure continually quoted by Roosevelt.

To the statement that the overwhelming majority of the press opposed Franklin Roosevelt, further qualification is necessary. There may be a need, as Frank Luther Mott has pointed out specifically in relation to the 1940 election, to disaggregate figures for newspaper opposition which lumped together the strident opposition of "bigoted party organs," in which headlines were biased, signed Washington correspondence unfair, and editorials and cartoons immoderate, with that of "reasonable partisans," which supported the candidate of their choice strongly, but reported fairly both sides of the campaign, and the "passive supporters" in which support for one candidate and opposition to the other tended to be nominal and phlegmatic. In 1940, according to Mott, the "bigoted party organs" were the smallest of the three groups, and the numbers of the "passive supporters" only slightly less than those of the "reasonable partisans," which comprised the largest class. One explanation for the relative lack of partisan political involvement of many newspapers, Mott has surmised, was that consolidations in the newspaper industry had, by 1940, greatly increased the number of communities which were served by a single newspaper, so that, in such circumstances, a newspaper which adopted a strongly partisan approach would run the risk of alienating a considerable section of its readership, and jeopardizing its local monopoly position.[4] Implicit in such an argument is the suggestion that, in the periods between presidential elections, the lukewarm allegiance given by the "passive supporters" to the president's opponents, as well as their opposition to him, might have all but melted away—in circumstances, that is, in which the need to make a specific declaration in favor of one presidential candidate or another no longer applied.

Whether for this or other reasons, statistics for press opposition to Roosevelt during election campaigns do not accurately reflect the editorial policies of the nation's press in the periods between elections. Two analyses of newspaper opinion, based on the editorial pages and front pages of newspapers in all sections of the United States and representing over 20 percent of total daily newspaper circulation, which found their way to the White House, provide some confirmation of this assertion. The first, which covered the week ending 7 October 1939, showed that the level of support for the president had been 50.0 percent in domestic affairs, 72.8 percent in foreign affairs, and that the weighted total of press treatment favorable to the administration had been 63.3 percent. The second survey, covering the week ending 20 April 1940, revealed a decline in press support for the administration's domestic policy to 24.4 percent, but a similarly high level of approval, 71.9 percent, for its foreign policies. The weighted total of newspaper support for the week covered by the second survey was 42.9 percent.[5]

An analysis, published by *Time* on 25 August 1941, of press support for Roosevelt over the two-year period from the outbreak of war and based on the weekly press surveys of editorial policies conducted by James S. Twohey Associates reinforces this point. That survey suggested that, over the period surveyed, Roosevelt typically won the approval of well above 50 percent of the nation's press for his handling of foreign issues; that his handling of domestic issues from August 1939 until the end of that year had been approved by something between 40 and 50 percent of the nation's press; that he had suffered a long period of press unpopularity in domestic affairs during 1940, with newspaper support running, on the average, at something approaching 30 percent; but that, following his reelection in November 1940, his domestic policies had been backed by, on the average, approximately 50 percent of the daily newspapers of America. The *Time* analysts commented that, on domestic issues, the president's popularity rose whenever he announced an economy move, took a strong stand against organized labor, or moved to control inflation; and that on foreign issues, his popularity with the press increased at times of crisis in the war (except during those periods when the plight of the Allies seemed hopeless), when trade treaties were negotiated, when he spoke to the nation on the radio, and when the United States was threatened by the Axis.

What such unofficial surveys revealed, the extensive sampling by the administration's own Division of Press Intelligence was repeatedly to confirm: day-to-day levels of press support for the Roosevelt administration far exceeded the levels prevailing during presidential election campaigns.

Direct evidence relating to press treatment of his administration reached Franklin Roosevelt from several sources: the surveys of the Democratic National Committee; his own daily newspaper reading; the results of analyses conducted by the Division of Press Intelligence; and the quantity of miscellaneous press clippings sent to him by associates and supporters.

In relation to the first of these sources, the results of a survey which Roosevelt himself commissioned from the Democratic National Committee during the election campaign of 1936 are of particular significance. [6] The survey examined 204 newspapers in cities of 100,000 people or more, not including those in the southern states, where, according to the compiler, Carl Byoir, "there is no contest."

	No. of Newspapers	Total Circulation
Pro-Roosevelt	50	6,462,814
Anti-Roosevelt	123	15,527,461
Independent	31	1,672,246
Total	**204**	**23,662,521**

Its results led Byoir to comment that: "On the whole, the percentage in favor of the President is . . . higher than any of us thought it would be," though he did point out that, of the total circulation of pro-Roosevelt newspapers of 6,462,814, a significant number, 2,500,000, were in New York alone, which meant that outside of that state there was a circulation, in large northern and western cities, of approximately 4,000,000 for the president and 13,000,000 against. Even with the predominantly pro-Roosevelt southern press excluded, however, the precentage of press opposition to the president revealed by the Democratic National Committee's own survey was 60, a result which does not approach the president's own frequently quoted figure of 85.

Roosevelt's contention that he faced overwhelming newspaper opposition may further be tested against the actual editorial treatment of his administrations by the newspapers which he read each day. [7] To assess this treatment, I made an examination of the editorial reactions of nine of those newspapers to a series of important events, distributed throughout Roosevelt's presidency and covering both domestic and foreign affairs. The events selected were as follows: Roosevelt's election in November 1932; his first Inaugural Address of March 1933; the first "fireside chat" in March 1933, in which he outlined measures to deal with the banking crisis; the end of the special session of Congress in June 1933 (the first hundred days); the message to Congress in February

1934, asking for legislation to regulate the Stock Exchange; the congressional elections of November 1934; the Supreme Court's invalidation of the NRA in May 1935; the "horse and buggy" press conference, at which Roosevelt attacked the Court's decision; the president's campaign address at Madison Square Garden on 31 October 1936; the election of November 1936; the second Inaugural Address of January 1937; Roosevelt's message of February 1937, on the reorganization of the Judiciary; the Quarantine Speech of October 1937; the "fireside chat" of June 1938, in which Roosevelt announced his intention to fight the "copperheads" in his own party; the decision of September 1939, to convene a special session of Congress, in order to seek the repeal of the arms embargo; Roosevelt's nomination for an unprecendented third term; the announcement, in September 1940, of the "destroyers for bases" deal; the election of November 1940; the third Inaugural Address of January 1941; the "fireside chat" of September 1942, in which Roosevelt threatened to act on price stabilization if Congress continued to refuse to do so; the Annual Message of January 1943; the acceptance by the president of the fourth-term nomination in July 1944; the election of November 1944; and the announcement of the Yalta Agreement in February 1945.

Editorials by the newspapers which Roosevelt read each day on these events were classified according to whether they were "favorable" to the administration, "unfavorable," or whether they constituted, in essence, a "general discussion" of the event in question, eschewing a strongly pro- or anti-administration line.[8] In order to test the reliability of my judgments as to the nature of the editorials, the results obtained from the analysis of three of the newspapers—the *New York Times*, the *Washington Post*, and the *Chicago Tribune*—were compared with the results obtained independently by another person.

Among the more important assumptions underlying these procedures were that, given his own newspaper-reading habits and the importance of the events in question, Roosevelt would have been aware of the nature of such editorial comment; that editorial reaction by the newspapers which he read each day to these critically important events might be expected to have significantly influenced his own attitudes toward the press as a whole, as well as to have provided a corrective should his own assessment of the editorial policies of the press in general be awry; that, in view of their obvious importance, these would have been issues which would have called for immediate editorial comment and about which editorial writers would have been unlikely to have been reticent; that such editorial comment would have been considered at the highest level, and would be likely, on that account, to uncover the basic sympathies of those who controlled editorial policies; and that, for these reasons, the editorials selected would constitute acid tests of the various newspapers' positions.

The results of the analysis of editorial opinion are shown in table 1. Of a total of 167 editorial comments by the newspapers which Roosevelt read each day on the issues selected, 55, or 33 percent, were favorable, 61, or 36.5 percent, were unfavorable, and 51, or 30.5 percent were general discussions of the issues in question. Among the individual newspapers surveyed, opposition came most obviously from the *Chicago Tribune*, which commented unfavorably on sixteen of the twenty occasions on which it offered editorial opinions on the issues examined, from the *New York Journal American*, a Hearst publication, which began in 1937, which criticized the president or his administration in four of the seven editorials which were surveyed, and from the *New York Sun*, which criticized Roosevelt on eleven of the twenty-two occasions on which it made an editorial comment on the issues in question. For only one other newspaper, the *New York Herald Tribune*, did the number of editorials critical of the president (seven) exceed the number which supported his actions (five). By contrast, of twenty-two editorials carried by the *Baltimore Sun*, eleven supported Roosevelt and five expressed opposition to him; of twenty-three editorials in the *Washington Post*, eleven were laudatory and six critical; of twenty-one editorials in the *New York World Telegram*, seven expressed support and four opposition; of twenty-three editorials in the *New York Times*, ten were supportive and five critical; and of nine editorial comments made by the *Washington Times Herald*, which began publication in 1939, five were favorable to Roosevelt and three unfavorable.

My judgments as to the character of the editorials carried by three of the newspapers in the sample accorded reasonably closely with those made independently by another person.[9] On the classifications for the

Table 1: Editorial Reaction by a Selected Group of Newspapers to Certain Events during Roosevelt's Presidency*

Election, 1932
First Inaugural Address, 1933
First fireside chat, 1933
End of special session of
    Congress, 1933
Stock Exchange regulation, 1934
Congressional elections, 1934
Invalidation NRA, 1935
"Horse and buggy" press
    conference, 1935
Campaign address, 1936
Election, 1936
Second Inaugural Address, 1937
Reorganization of
    Judiciary, 1937
Quarantine Speech, 1937
Fireside chat, 1938
Repeal of arms embargo, 1939
Third-term nomination, 1940
Destroyers for bases, 1940
Election, 1940
Third Inaugural, 1941
Fireside chat, 1942
Annual Message, 1943
Fourth-term nomination, 1944
Election, 1944
Yalta, 1945

Total
    Favorable
    Unfavorable
    General discussion

Newspapers

NYT	NYHT	CT	BS	WP	NYWT	NYS	NYJA	WTH	Total	F	U	GD
F	GD	GD	F	F	F	U			7	4	1	2
F	F	F	F	F	F	GD			7	6		1
F	...	...	F	F	...	F			4	4		
GD	...	U	F	GD	...	GD			5	1	1	3
GD	GD	...	na	GD	F	...			4	1		3
GD	GD	U	GD	GD	GD	GD			7	1		6
U	U	U	GD	U	F	U			7	1	5	1
...	...	...	U	U	...	...			2		2	
U	U	U	...	U	GD	U			6		5	1
F	GD	U	GD	GD	GD	U			7	1	2	4
F	GD	U	GD	U	GD	GD			7	1	2	4
U	U	U	U	U	U	U			7		7	
F	GD	U	F	F	F	U	U		8	4	3	1
GD	U	U	U	...	GD	U	...		6		4	2
F	F	U	F	F	GD	F	U	F	9	6	2	1
U	U	U	U	U	U	U	U	F	9	1	8	
GD	F	F	F	F	GD	U	...	F	8	5	1	2
GD	U	U	GD	GD	U	U	GD	F	9	2	3	4
F	GD	...	F	F	GD	F	GD	F	8	5		3
U	...	U	F	F	F	GD	...	NA	6	3	2	1
GD	F	U	F	F	F	GD	...	GD	8	4	1	3
GD	U	U	U	GD	U	U	U	U	9		7	2
F	GD	U	GD	F	GD	GD	GD	U	9	2	2	5
F	F	GD	F	F	GD	F	...	U	8	5	1	2
23	**20**	**20**	**22**	**23**	**21**	**22**	**7**	**9**	**167**			
10	5	2	11	11	7	4		5	55			
5	7	16	5	6	4	11	4	3	61			
8	8	2	6	6	10	7	3	1	51			

*NYT, New York Times; NYHT, New York Herald Tribune; CT, Chicago Tribune; BS, Baltimore Sun; WP, Washington Post; NYWT, New York World Telegram; NYS, New York Sun; NYJA, New York Journal American; WTH, Washington Times Herald; F, favorable comment; U, unfavorable comment; GD, general discussion; ellipses, no editorial; blank space, newspaper not published at that time (the New York Journal American began publication in 1937; the Washington Times Herald in 1939); NA, not available (in both cases, the relevant issues of the newspapers concerned were missing from the Library of Congress holdings).

twenty *Chicago Tribune* editorials, there was complete agreement; of the twenty-three editorials in the *Washington Post*, similar conclusions were reached in relation to nineteen; of twenty-three editorials published by the *New York Times*, there was disagreement, though not major disagreement, on seven, a discrepancy which may be accounted for by the fact that *Times* editorials often canvassed many sides of a particular question and qualified whatever conclusions were reached, making it more difficult to place editorials, with confidence, in one of the available categories. In this respect, among the nine newspapers examined, the *New York Times* was exceptional.

So far as the twenty-four events which were selected for the survey were concerned, on eleven of them—the election of 1932, the first Inaugural Address, the first "fireside chat," the Stock Exchange regulation plan, the Quarantine Speech, the move to repeal the arms embargo, the "destroyers for bases" deal, the third Inaugural Address, the threat to bypass Congress on price stabilization, the Annual Message of 1943, and the announcement of the Yalta Agreement in 1945—the balance as between favorable and unfavorable editorial comment went in the president's favor, usually heavily so. On a further eleven of the events selected—the result of the congressional elections in 1934, the invalidation of the NRA in 1935, the "horse and buggy" press conference, the campaign address of October 1936, the election of 1936, the second Inaugural Address, the announcement of the scheme to reorganize the Judiciary, the "fireside chat" of 1938, the third-term nomination, the election of 1940, and the fourth-term nomination in 1944—the balance of editorial comment went against the president, again, usually heavily so. On the remaining two events—the end of the special session of Congress in 1933 and the election of 1944—there was an even distribution of favorable and unfavorable editorial comment.[10]

Generally, the breakdown of editorial opinion suggests a pattern of early press enthusiasm for the New Deal, followed by a long trough of relative press unpopularity, extending from the decision of the Supreme Court invalidating the NRA in May 1935, to the period of intense debate over the Presidential Message on the reorganization of the Judiciary in February 1937; of strong subsequent opposition to Roosevelt's nomination for a third and then a fourth term; but of a consistently high level of support for the administration's major foreign policy initiatives.

No satisfactory confirmation of the assertion that the Roosevelt administration faced overwhelming opposition from the press is provided by such figures.

Further direct evidence as to the treatment of his administration by the press reached Roosevelt from the Division of Press Intelligence. This division was established in July 1933, by the direction of the president and at the instigation of Presidential Secretary Louis Howe. For a time, the division was operated as part of the NRA, but, in July 1935, was transferred to the National Emergency Council. When that agency was abolished in July 1939, the Division of Press Intelligence became part of the Office of Government Reports, until it was transferred, in June 1942, to the newly created Office of War Information. In November 1942, following a survey of its activities conducted by the Bureau of Intelligence of the Office of War Information and a budgetary cut imposed by Congress, the division's activities were sharply curtailed.

From the outset, the chief function of the Division of Press Intelligence was the reading and clipping by its staff of approximately four hundred of the largest daily newspapers in the United States and the preparation and distribution to government officials of a daily mimeographed bulletin, in which news and editorial comment on government activities were classified, briefly described, and indexed. From the vast reservoir of press clippings built up by the division, officials could be provided, on request, with clippings on news items of particular interest.

There were three vehicles through which the Division of Press Intelligence conveyed information concerning treatment by the daily press of the Roosevelt administration to the White House: the daily press intelligence bulletins; special reports on the editorial reaction to events which were considered to be of particular importance; and, from July 1941, until the effective emasculation of the division in November 1942, weekly summaries of the editorial reaction by the nation's press to foreign and domestic events.

The press intelligence bulletins[11] were lengthy and somewhat indigestible compilations, which classified news columns, editorial opinion, and the comments of the nation's columnists, and, through the provision of a numerical coding system, provided a means by which those receiving the bulletin could obtain copies of the various items included in summary form in the bulletin. Although the press intelligence bulletin was received each day at the White House, there is no evidence to show that the president made direct use of it, and, indeed, regular and detailed examination of the bulletins by him would almost certainly have been ruled out because of their size and the diverse and, to the president, marginally relevant nature of much of their content. Thus, for example, bulletin no. 80, issued on 30 December 1933, was over seventy pages in length and contained classifications of press comment on subjects ranging from monetary policy and local government to milk control, transient camps, and coast guard consolidation. Statistical breakdowns of editorial opinion, as distinct from news comment, on certain issues were occasionally provided. Bulletin no. 80, for instance, recorded that, of forty-four editorials on the president's silver-buying plan, in the papers covered by the division's survey during the preceding week, thirteen had been favorable, six unfavorable, and twenty-five had discussed the plan generally. The newspapers in which the various categories of editorial had appeared were then listed, along with index numbers which would have enabled them to be retrieved. Such surveys of editorial opinion may have been consulted by Roosevelt, though, considering the size of the bulletins and the frequency with which they appeared, it is not easy to conceive of this happening on a regular basis.

Of much greater use to the president would have been the occasional special reports of the Division of Press Intelligence.[12] To begin with, these reports took varying forms and appeared irregularly, sometimes being supplied on the initiative of the division's director, Katherine C. Blackburn, sometimes at the request of Roosevelt or of Stephen Early, who, on such occasions, was probably acting on the president's behalf.

One of the earliest of the special reports, which was received in January 1934, revealed that a recent speech by Roosevelt to a Woodrow Wilson Dinner had been commented on favorably in 130 editorials and unfavorably in 10. The report went on to list the newspapers which had carried favorable or unfavorable editorials and to reproduce typical excerpts. A month later, following a survey of the editorial reaction to

numerous speeches by Republicans on the occasion of Lincoln's birthday, which had severely criticized the administration, the Division of
Press Intelligence reported to the White House that most of the
speeches had not been commented on editorially, even by Republican
newspapers, and that, in Independent newspapers, the speakers had
been ridiculed. The compilers of the report went on to refer to overwhelming press criticism of Charles A. Lindbergh's telegram to the
president over the cancellation of airmail contracts, and to observe that
there was "not the slightest indication of any decrease in the tremendous
personal popularity of the President in every part of the nation."
Although the AAA was said to be receiving more editorial criticism
than any other part of the recovery program, the division's staff concluded that no outstanding critic of that program was commanding
national attention. A report which reached Stephen Early in April
1934, was less flattering and brought a terse comment from the press
secretary to the president: "You may be interested to know that an
editorial compilation made from a digest of 400 daily newspapers fails
to show a single editorial favorable to the proposed tax on coconut oil."
     Two lengthy memoranda on news and editorial comment on mea-
sures to be considered during the coming session of Congress, received
by the White House in November and December 1934, represented a
further attempt by its director to make the activities of the Divison of
Press Intelligence more directly useful to the president; but Roosevelt's
response to the innovation was tepid. More valuable than descriptive
and impressionistic surveys of this kind was a statistical breakdown of
editorial comment supplied by the division on two speeches on power,
delivered by the president in Tupelo, Mississippi, and Birmingham,
Alabama, on Sunday, 18 November 1934, which showed that twenty-
two newspapers had commented favorably on the speeches and eighteen
unfavorably. Like the reports on the measures which were to come
before Congress, this report was forwarded to Roosevelt.[13]
     If the early special reports sent by the Division of Press Intelligence
to the White House revealed a pattern of press response which was
predominantly favorable to the administration, considerable press opposition to several New Deal measures was indicated by a series of
analyses received during 1935. Thus, for instance, the balance of

editorial opinion was strongly against the Wagner Labor Disputes Bill, the Wheeler-Rayburn Utilities Holding Company Bill, the Steagall Banking Bill, and the Harrison NRA Extension Bill. Additionally, proposed AAA amendments were objected to on the ground that they would lead to "new dictatorial powers," the president's tax program was attacked and plans to continue the Public Works Art Project were disapproved. When the president asked for the passage of the editorially unpopular Guffey Coal Control Bill irrespective of doubts as to its constitutionality, the Division of Press Intelligence reported that his suggestion had been condemned by thirty-three of the newspapers sampled and endorsed by only four. At the end of May, a special memorandum on preliminary editorial reaction to the Supreme Court's invalidation of the NRA gave the president a foretaste of the overwhelming press endorsement which that decision was to receive.

Though of far less significance than the opposition to the New Deal domestic program, a measure of support for Roosevelt's policies was revealed by these same special reports. Thus, editorial comment on the president's message to Congress on the Utility and Holding Company Bill was shown to have been evenly balanced; the defeat of the Mc-Carran "prevailing wage" amendment was seen as a signal victory for the president; and the president's Ship Subsidy Message won support. Similarly, there was editorial approval of the SEC drive against "stock swindlers," and, in relation to the emergency relief program, lavish praise for the work done and for the assistance provided for the men involved. In the international sphere, too, the administration fared better: among newspapers which commented editorially, there was almost unanimous approval of the new reciprocal trade agreement with Russia and a measure of support for Secretary Hull's statement that, in its attitude to the Italian-Ethiopian controversy, the United States was concerned to preserve the Kellogg-Briand Pact.

The dominant tone of certain other special Division of Press Intelligence reports received at the White House during Roosevelt's first administration was more favorable. In May 1935, a report on editorial reaction to a statement on foreign trade, highly critical of the administration, issued by George N. Peek, was sent to the president at the request of the State Department. Its conclusion was that, while some anti-administration newspapers had viewed Peek's figures with the usual alarm and urged that an inquiry be launched into the foreign trade position, others, which were said by the division to have been consistently critical of the administration, had played down the issue. A second report, which reached the White House in May 1935, showed a balance of press comment in favor of the president on both domestic and foreign issues: a recent "fireside" radio broadcast had been commended by seventy-six newspapers and criticized by sixty-two; a United States Chamber of Commerce attack on the president's legislative program had been supported by forty-six newspapers but opposed by sixty-nine; Secretary Hull's efforts to revive foreign trade through reciprocal pacts had been widely praised; there had been a notable increase in favorable comment on the AAA program and "universal acclaim" for progress in reforestation. Additionally, the emergency conservation program had evoked unanimous praise, the expansion of the CCC had been generally approved, and, although there had been growing criticism of the planning of work relief organization, such criticism was still, the report concluded, outweighed by favorable sentiment. By contrast, attention was drawn to the existence of continuing heavy criticism of the cotton processing tax, the Steagall Banking Bill, and the New Deal recovery program.

In the area of foreign affairs, the Division of Press Intelligence recorded widespread press support for the president's proclamation of an arms embargo in October 1935. In a series of daily surveys covering the period from 21 October to 2 November, which Louis Howe directed the division to send to the president, editorial comment was shown to be heavily in Roosevelt's favor, with a total of thirty-four editorials praising the declaration, twenty-six disapproving of an attack made on it by the New York Port Development Conference, and twenty-three asking for an extension of the embargo to include materials such as cotton, copper, oil, and foodstuffs. No opposition to the proclamation was disclosed in the surveys.

In summary, the record of daily press treatment of the Roosevelt administration during the president's first term, as indicated in the special reports of the Division of Press Intelligence which reached the White House during that time, is one of strong initial support, of continued backing for the administration's foreign and trade policies, but of very substantial opposition to several New Deal agencies and to many aspects of the administration's legislative program, with relief and conservation policies standing as exceptions. In most cases, and possibly in all cases, the division's special reports which revealed these trends and characteristics were seen by the president.

The relatively few special reports from the Division of Press Intelligence which the White House received during Roosevelt's second term gave some confirmation of these trends of substantial, though by no means unqualified, press opposition to the administration's domestic program and continued support for its stand on foreign affairs. In June 1937, an analysis of press reaction to the president's Message to Congress proposing minimum wage and maximum hours legislation revealed a mixed editorial response, the objectives of the message meeting with "widespread indorsement," but the means by which those objectives were to be attained, namely, the Black-Connery Labor Standards Bill, encountering "almost unanimous denunciation." More favorable to the administration were the results of a survey by the division of press reaction to the president's Annual Message in 1938: of 142 editorials devoted to the address in its entirety, sixty-nine had endorsed it, fifty-two had criticized it, and twenty-one had discussed it in general terms. However, when the president argued directly, in a speech to the American Retail Forum in May 1938, for a continuation of New Deal policies and objectives, Press Secretary Stephen Early forwarded to him a special report of the division which showed that, of 219 editorials on the address, only eighteen had definitely applauded the president's stand. Of the remainder, 150 had opposed it and fifty-one had discussed the speech in general terms. Continuance of general press support for the administration's foreign policy was indicated in a memorandum which revealed that, of the newspapers sampled by the Division of Press Intelligence during the period from 1 May to 1 June 1940, eighty-three had published editorials in favor of granting aid to the allies, as against forty-nine which had expressed opposition to such a move.[14]

The reporting to the president by the Division of Press Intelligence became systematized during Roosevelt's third term. In July 1941,

Lowell Mellett, director of the Office of Government Reports, of which the division had become a part, offered to provide the president with weekly statistical abstracts of editorial opinion, as prepared by the division from the press intelligence bulletins compiled over that period. Roosevelt accepted the offer. Described by Mellett as "a more careful and complete check of editorial opinion than is being made by any other agency, private or governmental," these weekly reports presented, in concise and readily usable form, a statistical breakdown of editorial opinion of the nation's press on a wide variety of subjects, foreign and domestic. Moreover, because many of the statistics were cumulative, these weekly reports would have enabled the president to watch the shifts in editorial opinion on important issues.[15]

On example was the question of the extension of the term of military service for selectees, National Guardsmen, and Reserves, editorial opinion on which was monitored weekly from 14 July to 21 August 1941. The proposal had received overwhelming endorsement.

Another subject which was treated in considerable detail in early reports was that of United States–Japanese relations. Editorial opinion on this issue, as monitored by the division, revealed a widespread demand for firm action by the United States in the current crisis, embracing such measures as the freezing of Japanese assets, and stern criticism of the past policy of appeasement. Weekly summaries during August and September showed a strongly favorable editorial reaction to the Roosevelt-Churchill conference and the Atlantic Charter declaration, while isolationist sentiment was shown to be on the wane when a radio speech by the president in early September earned widespread approval, while a speech by Charles Lindbergh at Des Moines on the same evening was the subject of bitter press criticism.

In domestic affairs, two matters which figured prominently in the early weekly reports of the division, which were sent to the White House, were the administration's tax bill and the proposed legislation to control prices and installment buying. The former had received a mixed editorial response; the latter, broad support.

In addition to the breakdowns of editorial opinion on various subjects, early copies of the weekly reports included miscellaneous sections, under which were collected news items that, the Division of Press

Intelligence analysts evidently believed, might have been of particular interest to the president. Thus, for example, there was included in the summary covering the period from 5 to 14 August 1941, a report on an article by W. Kelsy, from the *Detroit News* of 7 August, which had linked Roosevelt's "disappearance" on his trip to meet Churchill with the mysterious trip of Cleveland on the yacht *Oneida* in 1893, during which, it was discovered, a team of five surgeons had operated on a malignant ulcer in the roof of Cleveland's mouth. Kelsy's story hinted at a similar explanation for Roosevelt's absence. Another item in this issue reported on a news story in the *Chicago Tribune*, which reviewed the application made by pro-New Deal publisher J. David Stern to the Reconstruction Finance Corporation for a loan, the refusal of the application, the subsequent intervention by Hopkins and Corcoran, and the eventual arrangement of the loan through Philadelphia and Canadian banks. An editor's footnote to the story read: "Another story of how the public purse was used to control a newspaper will be published soon."

The system of reporting by the Division of Press Intelligence reached its highest stage of development during the period from 26 September 1941 to 15 May 1942. During that time, the weekly reports which Roosevelt received commenced with a crisp and lucid two-page summary of the salient features of the week's editorial opinion. Containing interpretative as well as purely analytical comment, these skillfully devised preliminary comments would have enabled the president to see, virtually at a glance, what the general drift of newspaper opinion in the United States was and how press opinion was dividing on crucial domestic and foreign issues.[16]

In the period from the inception of these summaries to the attack on Pearl Harbor, editorial opinion on international affairs reflected a further strengthening of press support for the administration's foreign policy. The analysis for the week 19 to 25 September 1941, which set the general tone of what was to follow, pointed out that recent events abroad, notably the reports from Russia and continued sinking of ships, had had a marked effect in unifying the press in support of more aggressive action and stronger support for the president's foreign policy. The administration's policy of "aiding the democracies" was being strongly backed, with a majority of newspapers urging the prompt granting of additional Lend-Lease funds. Condemnation of isolationists in general and of Lindbergh in particular had risen sharply.

Over following weeks the summaries revealed strong and growing support for the president's request for revision of the Neutrality Acts, and for the proposal to arm merchant ships, as well as continuing acceptance of the need for additional Lend-Lease funds and rising hostility to isolationist policies. When the United States-Japanese crisis developed in November 1941, the Division of Press Intelligence reported "virtual unanimity in support of the handling of the situation by Secretary Hull and an insistent demand that we stand firm against appeasement or too great compromise."

The prefatory summaries of weekly Division of Press Intelligence reports in the period from 26 September to the outbreak of the war with Japan dealt with domestic affairs and the national defense effort, as well as the foreign situation. The preliminary summary of the report covering the period 19 to 25 September noted that the Supply Priorities Allocations Board was receiving a divided press, that there was overwhelming press criticism of Secretary Ickes' handling of the oil shortage situation, and that a majority of the press had approved the administration's tax bill, but was demanding an urgent curtailment of non-defense expenditures. The report drew attention, also, to strong press criticism of the president for reviving the controversy over the Supreme Court, through the publication of an article in *Collier's*. Over succeeding weeks, Secretary Morgenthau was commended for warning of the dangers of inflation but repeatedly criticized over a proposal to place a 100 percent tax on profits in excess of 6 percent, and the NYC and CCC were attacked for high-pressure recruiting tactics aimed at maintaining their allocations of funds. While the past achievements of both agencies were recognized, sharp curtailment of their activities was now urged. In another sphere of domestic policy, there was general editorial support for the admininstration's proposal to restrict installment buying and qualified support for the scheme to control prices, general agreement on the necessity for price control being coupled with a widespread insistence that such control be extended to cover wages and farm prices. The summaries drew attention, also, to the overwhelming press condemnation of John L. Lewis for calling the captive coal miners' strike in defiance of the president, though such condemnation was accompanied by much editorial criticism of Secretary Perkins and administration labor policies, which were held by many newspapers to be accountable for the existing labor crisis. The dispute having been settled, the president won editorial praise for his patience and success in the handling of it.

Predictably, the Japanese attack on Pearl Harbor was followed by an upsurge of patriotic sentiment in the nation's press. Division of Press Intelligence reports reaching the president in the early weeks of the war revealed that his message to Congress asking for a declaration of war against Japan, his radio address to the nation on 9 December, and his talks with Churchill aimed at formulating a unified Allied command had received wholehearted editorial endorsement. Even Secretary Knox's report on Pearl Harbor was generally commended for its frankness. Similarly, the division's survey of editorial opinion for the week ending 31 December 1941, referred to "almost unanimous agreement on major international and war issues." To convey an impression of the sentiment aroused by the president's Annual Message, delivered the following week, the division included representative excerpts from various editorials in the preliminary section of its report: "equal to this hour of destiny" (*Baltimore Sun*), "fiercely inspiring" (*New York Mirror*), "summons...to total victory" (*Philadelphia Bulletin*), "call to toil and battle" (*New York Herald Tribune*), "fighting speech" (*Washington Post*), "ringing speech" (*Philadelphia Inquirer*), and, from the *Wall Street Journal*, "Okeh, Mr. President, let's go."

Such enthusiasm continued throughout the early part of 1942, the president's radio address to the nation in mid-February evoking "practically unanimous editorial praise and endorsement," although a report reaching the White House early in March did refer to "continued and growing criticism" of the Allies' relations with Vichy France.

During the period from the Japanese attack on Pearl Harbor to November 1942, at which time the Division of Press Intelligence's activities were sharply curtailed, the general pattern of weekly reports continued to be one of strong editorial endorsement for the president's major public pronouncements on war issues, coupled with a continuing commentary on domestic affairs and the defense effort (the line between which, in the division's reports, had become blurred), which was critical but not overwhelmingly so. From time to time, substantial press hostility was directed against shortcomings in the war effort, with recurring charges of inefficiency and disunity with the administration, and toward the continuation into wartime of the activities of certain New Deal agencies, especially the CCC and the NYA, now thought to be inappropriate. On the other hand, there was considerable newspaper backing for the administration's attempts to institute price and installment buying control, though, in relation to the former, the lack of control over wages and farm prices continued to cause discontent, and qualified support for the administration's production, labor, and taxation policies.

Neither on the basis of the regular reports from the Division of Press Intelligence which were received during the period from July 1941 to November 1942, nor on the basis of the special reports received by Roosevelt during his first and second terms, can the charge of overwhelming newspaper opposition to his administrations be sustained.

About the final major source of direct information concerning press treatment of his administration which Roosevelt received—the press clippings sent to him by supporters and associates—it is difficult to generalize, for, unless such clippings were earmarked, on arrival, for inclusion in one of the special subject files within the president's personal file, the president's official file, or the papers of Press Secretary Stephen Early, they would have vanished, beyond the limits of feasible search, into the vastitudes of alphabetically filed presidential mail.

So far as hostile press clippings are concerned, the great bulk of those which are recoverable were taken from the *Chicago Tribune* and the Hearst press. One sample of anti-*Tribune* mail received by Roosevelt was a letter from Charles A. Churan, dated 6 November 1933, complaining that a *Tribune* cartoon of that date was "a cowardly, traiterous [sic] act" and was "maliciously untruthful." Another letter, of which Roosevelt received a copy, told the editor of the *Tribune*: "At present you are conducting a most vicious, damnable, and contemptuous [sic?] campaign against the GREATEST PRESIDENT, [sic] who ever occupied the White House."[17] Among the favorable clippings received by the president were a large number of editorials written by the pro-administration and anti-*Tribune* editor of the *Chicago Daily Times*, Richard Finnegan. In May 1935, for example, the paper's managing editor, Louis Ruppel, sent to Roosevelt one of Finnegan's editorials, which, he asserted, was "as fine a piece of work as I have ever seen." A grateful president requested Ruppel to tell Finnegan, on his behalf, "that that editorial is the kind that helps a fellow!" Nor was it unusual for the supportive editorials of William Allen White to be brought to the president's attention.[18]

While it is not too difficult to believe that hostile and sometimes abusive clippings from McCormick and Hearst publications may have impressed themselves more firmly on Roosevelt's mind than did clippings which indicated newspaper support, it appears that, of the clippings which found their way into the papers of Roosevelt and Early, the number which expressed opposition to Roosevelt may not have exceeded, on a straight quantitative basis, the number which expressed support.

The notion that Franklin Roosevelt was opposed by the overwhelming majority of the press became established as part of New Deal conventional wisdom and has survived to become part of its legend. Testimony on this point from contemporaries is as unanimous as it is unreliable: Presidential Assistant Samuel Rosenman wrote in relation to the 1936 campaign that "at least 85 per cent of the press was against him [Roosevelt]"; Democratic National Committee Director of Publicity Charles Michelson asserted, in relation to the elections of 1936 and 1940, that "nearly all papers were anti-Roosevelt"; pro-New Deal publisher J. David Stern believed that 90 percent of the press opposed the president in 1936, a figure quoted also by reporter Charles Hurd, specifically in relation to the 1940 election, and by Justice William O. Douglas and Rexford Tugwell in general comments on the New Deal period made in recent correspondence with me.[19]

The actual situation was significantly different. So far as the declared political affiliation of the nation's daily newspapers was concerned, the number of Republican and Independent-Republican publications probably never amounted, during Roosevelt's presidency, to more than 30 percent of the total of daily newspapers. That, in addition to these, some Independent and Independent-Democratic newspapers opposed Roosevelt is undeniable; that all of them did so, together with a not insignificant proportion of nominally Democratic newspapers, is inconceivable. In relation to presidential election campaigns, when newspaper opposition to Franklin Roosevelt reached its peak, it is only by equating "absence of support" with "opposition," and by lumping together those newspapers which remained uncommitted to either candidate with those who opposed the New Deal, that Roosevelt's estimate of the magnitude of press opposition to the New Deal may be approximated. During the periods between elections, it is clear, press opposition to the Roosevelt administration fell well below its presidential campaign level.

The general pattern of daily newspaper treatment of the Roosevelt administration, a pattern which is suggested by the results of the editorial survey discussed above and confirmed by reports from the Division of Press Intelligence, is one of strong support for the early New Deal program; general, and, at times, bitter, though by no means unqualified opposition to the president's domestic policies; widespread opposition to certain events, such as the attempt to reorganize the Judiciary and the third-term bid; and continuing support for Roosevelt's foreign and defense policies. The material from which such a pattern of press treatment could have been built up was made available to Roosevelt through his own daily newspaper reading, through the special and weekly reports of the Division of Press Intelligence, from at least one important survey by the Democratic National Committee, and (although it is not possible to be as confident on this point) from the press clippings sent to him by supporters and associates. Of the general nature of that pattern, Roosevelt could scarcely have been ignorant.

"Remember this always," the president told representatives of the American Youth Conference at a press conference with them on 5 June 1940, "85 percent of the papers of the United States are opposed to this Administration." Although others besides Franklin Roosevelt would make the charge, he, far more than they, had grounds for knowing it to be false.

Five

His Displeasure, like the Rain,
Falls Equally upon the Just and the Unjust

However much he may have regretted the lack of newspaper support for his policies, Franklin Roosevelt's frequently voiced objections to the press of America had less to do with its editorial policy than with its ethics. In this respect, it is clear, his chief concern was with the question of bias in the presentation of news. The opposition of newspaper owners might legitimately be expressed through statements of newspaper opinion, but when, as Roosevelt believed was consistently the case, it overflowed the editorial columns to produce a distortion of news presentation, such opposition threatened not merely the freedom of the press, but, since it destroyed public confidence in the reliability of the sources of information, the future of the American democratic system as well. No less an indication than editorial opposition of overwhelming proprietor-hostility, the widespread distortion of news by the press of the United States was, Franklin Roosevelt believed, more threatening and more insidious.

Clearly, to make a general assessment of the ethical standards of the press during the presidency of Franklin Roosevelt would be a daunting and excessively difficult task. In the swirl of contemporary debate about that institution views are polarized, criteria subjective and ill-defined, examples always striking but usually extreme; so that it is not easy to see where the balance of the argument lies. For every thrust, there is a parry: if the president asserts that newspapers, too frequently edited from the counting room, are losing the confidence of the people, William Allen White, speaking to the American Society of Newspaper Editors in 1939, declares that "the American press is honest according to its lights, which are clearer and more penetrating than the illumination of any other section of American public life," and adds defiantly: "We invite comparison in our conduct and morals with the politicians who run our government."[1]

Just as general criticism of the press in the age of Roosevelt may be found in rich profusion, particular examples of press misdemeanors may be accumulated to the point of tedium. Some were dramatically publicized by the White House itself. At his press conference on 18 May 1937, Roosevelt told the correspondents of two messages sent by the McClure Syndicate to its subscribers: the first referred to a report by an unnamed medical specialist that Roosevelt had been found at his desk in a coma; the second repeated assertions by the head of a large corporation that "the paranoic in the White House" was destroying America and that "a couple of well-placed bullets would be the best thing for the country." A further example was contained in a White House statement, issued in August 1935, which reproduced a copy of a message dispatched recently to all Hearst editors and Universal Service Bureaus. The message read:

> The Chief [Hearst] instructs that the phrase "SOAK THE SUC-CESSFUL" be used in all references to the Administration's Tax Program instead of the phrase "SOAK THE THRIFTY" hitherto used, also he wants the words "RAW DEAL" used instead of "NEW DEAL."

Such an instruction, the White House pointed out, amounted to "the deliberate coloring of so-called news stories, in accordance with orders issued to those responsible for the writing of news."[2] More caustically, *Nation*, of 28 August 1935, observed that readers of Hearst editorials should find it enlightening "to learn that their daily journalistic bread is baked, sliced, and poisoned in a central office in New York." The Hearst instruction represented the clearest possible illustration of the kind of owner-inspired news distortion of which Roosevelt complained.

Nor is it uncommon, in the literature of the period, to find complaints that the comments of syndicated columnists had been omitted or selectively pruned in accordance with the predilections of their clients. Why, *Nation* publicly asked Roy Howard in its issue of 14 May 1938, had a column by Westbrook Pegler, which expressed sympathy for Spanish Loyalists, been omitted from the *New York World Tele-gram*? Why had an appeal by Heywood Broun for penny postcards to be sent to Congress in support of the president's recovery program been removed from his column after the first edition? Why, when Raymond Clapper attacked Roosevelt's critics during the reorganization struggle, was his column altered so that it reflected unfavorably on the president? Later, New Deal partisan Walter Winchell, chagrined by the fact that nine of the twenty-eight columns which he had submitted in a single month to Eleanor Patterson's *Washington Times Herald* had been suppressed, inserted an advertisement in the rival *Washington News*:

> Attention Mr. and Mrs. Washington, D.C.: A certain Washington newspaper whose initials are T.H. omits considerable material from the column I write. . . . The omissions were usually about certain so-called Americans—pro-Nazis and pro-Japs.[3]

On another occasion, Roosevelt himself intervened on behalf of pro-New Deal columnist Jay Franklin, whose column had been dropped by two newspapers owned by J. David Stern.[4]

In any history of press ethics in the presidency of Franklin Roosevelt, the Hearst press would merit a special chapter. The tone and style of its opposition to Roosevelt may readily be appreciated: a Hearst attack, in 1936, on the WPA was headed "Taxpayers Feed 20,000 Reds on N.Y. Relief Rolls"; Hearst reporters were prevented, in the closing stages of the campaign of that year, from writing anything which suggested that the reelection of Roosevelt was a possibility; in October 1936, in the *New York American*, Hearst referred to the president and his associates as "you and your fellow Communists"; included in the same issue of this newspaper was a poem which began:

> A Red New Deal with a Soviet seal
> Endorsed by a Moscow hand,
> The strange result of an alien cult
> In a liberty-loving land.[5]

The more bizarre exploits of the Hearst organization were often exposed by the chain's journalistic rivals. In 1938, when Hearst publications promoted the idea of special "Paul Revere" trains to carry disgruntled citizens to Washington to protest against "the dictator bill" (a Roosevelt measure aimed at government reorganization), Hearst's *Chicago Herald and Examiner* referred enthusiastically to "a great cross section of Chicago and Illinois" which had gathered for the journey; but, when the special rail cars departed the following day, the *Chicago Daily News* estimated that only 350 Paul Reveres had rallied to the call, while a reporter from the pro-New Deal *Chicago Daily Times*, who searched the trains, was unable to find any. Subsequent inquiry by the *Times* did locate one man who had made the trip. "His name is Morris Stein," reported the newspaper solemnly. "He sells fruit and vegetables."[6]

As blatant as anything produced by the Hearst press was the tendentious treatment of news by Colonel Robert McCormick's *Chicago Tribune*. Examples abound: for more than a week of the presidential campaign of 1936, the *Tribune* alluded to Roosevelt only once on its front page; when unedifying practices were discovered in two Wisconsin cities, the newspaper headed its report: "Roosevelt Area in Wisconsin Is Hotbed of Vice."[7] At whatever point its output is sampled, the quality of the *Tribune* seems similar. The front page of the issue of 2 November 1940, chosen at random from those produced during the campaign of that year, is instructive. A banner headline, "Flaw in Draft Lottery Told," introduces a report that two eminent Chicago mathematicians had branded the existing lottery system for military selection unfair; other page-one headlines proclaim: "Willkie Blames Roosevelt for Lack of Planes," "Business Ready for Prosperity if Willkie Wins," "G.O.P. Seeking a Dictatorship, Says Roosevelt," and "Political Hoodlums Hit Republicans with Violence and Threats." Also on page one is a dispatch ("Federal Agents Quiz Ohioan for Wiring F.D.R.") which claims that a man who sent a telegram to the president protesting an order which conferred a captaincy on Roosevelt's son, Elliott, has been visited by Secret Service agents and "threatened with reprisal, if the incident was repeated," and a story of an alleged attack by Mayor LaGuardia on a bystander at an election rally, to which the mayor had gone to speak in support of the president ("Detroit Questioner He Roughed up Sues 'The Little Flower' "). A cartoon features a

giant ballot paper, in the form of a stone slab, on which the space
marked "Roosevelt" is being marked with an "X." Under the slab is a
large crucifix labeled "war," beneath which a tangle of soldiers is being
pitilessly crushed. The cartoon carries the suggestive caption: "A Cross
for the Backs of Your Sons."

As well as being suppressed and distorted, news was also invented.
On 9 August 1936, under the screaming headline "Moscow Orders
Reds in U.S. to Back Roosevelt," the *Tribune* carried a report from its
northern European correspondent, Donald Day, that the Russian
Communist party had directed its American counterpart to support
Roosevelt and work to defeat his opponent, characterized in the dispatch as a representative of "forces which opposed the development of
class war and revolution in America." The origin of the story was later
shown by the rival *Chicago Daily News*, which exposed the hoax, to
have been a speech by Earl Browder, general secretary of the American
Communist party, delivered the previous May. Browder's remarks had
been reprinted by the Soviet journal *Kommunistieceski International*,
from which, in turn, the Day dispatch had been drawn. When, later in
the campaign, the president visited Chicago for an election rally, the
Tribune featured a front-page picture of a man collecting discarded
Roosevelt campaign buttons from the street. But the collector, a rival
newspaper discovered, had been paid for his services by the *Tribune*,
and the buttons had been supplied by that newspaper's own
photographer.[8]

But although such dubious chapters in the history of the press during
the Roosevelt presidency need to be written, that history itself was
something more than a shameful chronicle of news distortion and
journalistic excess. Significant, in this respect, are several indications
that the press had not forfeited the confidence of the public at large. A
Gallup poll in January 1938 found that 73 percent of those surveyed felt
that newspapers were fair to the Roosevelt administration, as against
27 percent who believed them to be unfair. Eighty-five percent of
Republican respondents answered in the affirmative, but so did 65
percent of the Democrats. A second Gallup poll in October of that year
found 82 percent of respondents agreeing with the proposition that the
news columns in the newspaper of their choice treated the administra-

tion fairly.[9] The following year, the August edition of *Fortune* carried the results of an extensive survey of public attitudes toward the press conducted by the Elmo Roper organization. Of those surveyed, 23.3 percent agreed that the news was "almost always accurate as to its facts," a further 45.1 percent affirmed that it was usually accurate (a total of 68.4 percent for these two categories), while 24.7 percent thought it "not accurate in many instances." Asked, further, whether they believed that the newspapers which they read had been too friendly or too antagonistic toward the president, 12.9 percent considered that they had been too friendly, 23.1 percent too antagonistic, while 48.2 percent agreed with neither proposition and 15.8 percent had no opinion. *Fortune* concluded that a net balance of 10.2 percent believed that the press had been too hostile to Franklin Roosevelt.

These general conclusions were supported by Dr. George Gallup in comments which he made on a survey of public attitudes toward newspapers carried out by the American Institute of Public Opinion during the 1940 election campaign. Evidence from the survey, he declared, "indicates that, by and large, the newspaper readers of the country are satisfied that the press is fair and unbiased in its handling of political news." Fifty-four percent of those surveyed believed that the newspapers they read regularly had given Roosevelt and Willkie an "even break" during the campaign, 36 percent believed that they had not, and 10 percent were unable to offer an opinion. Of the group comprising the 36 percent, three-quarters indicated that Willkie had been favored by their newspapers. Fifty-one percent of Roosevelt voters believed that their newspapers had been objective, as against 60 percent of Willkie voters; 41 percent of Roosevelt voters thought that their newspapers had not given the two candidates equal treatment, as against 33 percent of Willkie voters. On the other hand, 75 percent of respondents regarded their newspapers as being fair in their treatment of the Roosevelt administration outside of election years, as against 12 percent who did not, and 13 percent who did not know. Eighty-one percent of Willkie voters answered this question in the affirmative, but so did 72 percent of Roosevelt supporters.[10]

The extent of proprietorial influence over the reporting of news, another matter on which Roosevelt made confident pronouncements, was one of the questions investigated by Leo Rosten in his survey of the Washington press in 1935. Rosten discovered that, although a majority of reporters (roughly 60 percent) were aware of the policies of the newspapers for which they worked, those policies were rarely enforced by orders from the home office. They were maintained, rather, through "less conscious and more subtle channels: through a choice of personnel, through subjective adjustments on the part of reporters, and through the institutionalization of a scale of values within the organization." Rosten's findings do not support the idea that reporters were ordered, in an explicit way, to slant their dispatches in a manner which was unfavorable to the Roosevelt administration.[11]

Indeed, that charge was explicitly and vigorously denied, on many occasions, by the reporters themselves. "To hazard a percentage," United Press White House correspondent Merriman Smith has written, "Mr. Roosevelt was wrong more than 90 per cent about story slanting." Smith went on to assert that "not to my knowledge have I ever been 'ordered' to ask a question or slant a story by any newspaper boss in my life, from the United Press on down to the *Athens* (Georgia) *Daily Times.*" And, he added emphatically, "The first time a boss says, 'Here, let's do a job on this guy regardless of the facts,' then I go back to my old job as night clerk of the Pulaski House in Savannah, Georgia."[12] Essentially the same point was made by newsman Walter Davenport in a comment on Roosevelt's charge that reporters frequently had to write as they were instructed on pain of losing their jobs. "Nothing that Mr. Roosevelt says," Davenport wrote in *Collier's* of 3 February 1945, "fetches more sustained denials from the correspondents than this."

If the problem of arriving at an assessment of the general ethical standard of the press during the presidency of Franklin Roosevelt is excessively difficult, the task at hand is, fortunately, a good deal simpler. For the concern of the present inquiry is not so much with the ethics of the press in general, as with the ethics of that section of the press of which Franklin Roosevelt had direct and reliable knowledge, and, more specifically, with an evaluation of the major criticisms which Roosevelt made of press ethics (and especially of his repeated assertion that stories were slanted against his administration on the orders of newspaper owners) in the light of the evidence relating to those criticisms of which he was aware.

Such evidence came, in the main, from press clippings and other information collected independently by the White House, or sent to the president by supporters and associates, and from Roosevelt's own extensive daily newspaper reading. So far as the first is concerned, Secretary Early maintained special files, with titles such as "Below the Belt," or "A.P.—News Stories Showing Distinct Bias Against the President and the Administration 1936–1938," in which examples of press misdemeanors were collected.[13] Various reports in the latter file were criticized by the press secretary for being "without foundation," for being "slanted," for employing "free phraseology," for revealing "evil political intent...toward the Administration," or, in another instance, for seeing in a serious news story only "an opportunity to be funny or facetious and to hold the President up to public ridicule." Thus, for example, a dispatch from the Associated Press carried by the *Washington Post* on 18 June 1938, began:

> The noted team of Corcoran and Cohen was hard at work yesterday trying to rescue the Administration from a power policy snarl. . . . The job entrusted to the two young Roosevelt admirers. . . is full of political dynamite.

Describing the report as "more of an editorial than a news story," Early enquired of the two members of the administration referred to in it whether the information in the dispatch was accurate. Their answer was that it was not. Roosevelt also asked Early to check periodically on the reporting of the United Press so that "they may know they are being watched, if for no other reason."[14]

Material from the collection of journalistic transgressions by the Associated Press became the basis for a series of complaints made personally to Robert McLean, its president, at a private meeting with Roosevelt in October 1938. Having made his general charges, the president then invited McLean to discuss with Stephen Early the contents of the file of offending clippings which the White House had assembled.[15]

In addition to such information about press behavior, of which

Roosevelt, presumably, would have been made generally aware, many letters of complaint about press practices were sent to the president. Of those which found their way into the papers of the president or of his press secretary, the great bulk related to the practices of McCormick and Hearst publications, and to what were considered to be unpatriotic activities by certain sections of the press during the war. ("May I ask," wrote an impassioned supporter in March 1942, "why you allow these frightful publications to continue to be printed and circulated among our people? This is not free speech. It is free suicide for our beloved country.")[16] A proportion of such letters would have been seen by Roosevelt. But the most systematic information on the treatment of news by the nation's press reached Roosevelt through his extensive daily newspaper reading.

To test, against the evidence derived from that source, the validity of Roosevelt's charges of widespread news distortion in the press, I constructed two comparative analyses. In the first, the texts of three important speeches made by the president during the 1936 presidential campaign and three important speeches made during the 1940 campaign were compared with the actual reporting of those speeches by the newspapers which Roosevelt read each day. In the second, a comparison was made between the actual transcripts of the president's White House press conferences over the three-month periods before the 1936 and 1940 elections with the front-page reporting of these press conferences by the newspapers which Roosevelt read each day. Press conferences held during presidential trips within these three-month periods were excluded from the sample because only a minority of the newspapers which Roosevelt read each day sent representatives to cover such trips.[17]

Among the assumptions underlying these procedures were that a comparison between the actual and the reported would make the detection of story slanting relatively simple and would greatly reduce the subjective element involved in evaluating the news reports in question; that a comparison of the treatment of the same speech or press conference by several newspapers would tend to throw instances of story slanting into sharp relief; that, if news distortion occurred, it would mostly likely have taken place in the period preceding these bitterly contested elections; that, on this account, the treatment of these important presidential utterances would provide acid tests of the journalistic standards of the newspapers concerned; that, notwithstanding the preceding point, the reports sampled might be expected to be more generally representative of the standards of news reporting which prevailed in the newspapers examined. It was assumed, further, that Roosevelt would probably have seen the reports in question, and that such reports might be expected to have influenced his ideas on the prevalence or otherwise of news distortion in the nation's press.

In relation to each newspaper's reporting of each speech and each press conference, the following questions were posed: was the report, in terms of headlining and of selection and presentation of news, fair and accurate? Assuming this *not* to have been the case, then in relation to newspaper accounts which showed a degree of bias *against* the president, was such bias (1) relatively mild, (2) serious? And, in relation to newspaper accounts which showed a degree of bias *in favor* of the president, was such bias (1) relatively mild, (2) serious? The results of the analyses of three of the newspapers—the *New York Times*, the *Washington Post*, and the *Chicago Tribune*—have been compared with those obtained, independently, by another person.

The speeches selected for comparative examination were, for the period of the 1936 presidential election: the address by Roosevelt to the Democratic State Convention at Syracuse, New York, on 29 September; the radio address, on 23 October, to dinners of businessmen held throughout the nation; and the campaign address at Madison Square Garden on 31 October; and, for the period of the 1940 election: the president's address to the Teamsters' Union Convention, Washington, D.C., on 11 September, his address on hemisphere defense, at Dayton, Ohio, on 12 October; and his radio address to the *New York Herald Tribune* Forum, on 24 October. The results of the analysis of the newspaper treatment of these speeches are shown in table 2.

Of a total of forty-seven examples of newspaper treatment of Roosevelt's speeches which were examined, twenty-six were fair and accurate reports of the president's remarks, three were mildly biased in his favor, five were mildly biased against him, and thirteen seriously biased against him. A comparison of the gradings for the reporting of the

Table 2:   Reporting of Roosevelt's Speeches by Nine Newspapers during 1936 and 1940 Election Campaigns*

Speeches	Newspapers								
1936	*NYT*	*NYHT*	*CT*	*BS*	*WP*	*NYWT*	*NYS*	*NYJA*	*WTH*
29 September	F	F	− M	F	F	F	− M		
23 October	F	F	− S	F	F	− M	− S		
31 October	F	− S	− S	+ M	+ M	NA	− S		
1940									
11 September	F	− M	− S	F	F	− S	− S	− S	F
12 October	F	F	− M	F	F	− S	− S	F	+ M
24 October	F	F	F	F	F	− S	− S	F	F

*NYT, New York Times; NYHT, New York Herald Tribune; CT, Chicago Tribune; BS, Baltimore Sun; WP, Washington Post; NYWT, New York World Telegram; NYS, New York Sun; NYJA, New York Journal American; WTH, Washington Times Herald. In all cases, the reports were contained in the first editions of these newspapers to be published after the speeches. Texts of all speeches were printed by the New York Times on the days on which the speeches were reported. F, reporting fair and accurate; − M, mildly biased against the president; − S, seriously biased against the president; + M, mildly biased in favor of the president; + S, seriously biased in favor of the president; NA, not available (the issue of the New York World Telegram in which Roosevelt's speech of 31 October 1936 would have been reported is missing from the holdings of this newspaper in the New York Public Library); blank space, newspaper not being published at that time.

presidential speeches by three of the newspapers in the sample—the *New York Times*, the *Washington Post*, and the *Chicago Tribune*—with those made independently by another person revealed a wide measure of agreement, with five of the six reports by each of the three newspapers in question being graded similarly.[18]

So far, at least, as their reporting of the six speeches in question was concerned, three of the newspapers which Roosevelt read each day—the *Baltimore Sun*, the *Washington Post*, and the *New York Times*—maintained consistently high journalistic standards. The *Baltimore*

Sun's accounts of five of the six presidential speeches came close to Roosevelt's ideal of straight, factual reporting. In the remaining speech, the occasional interpolation of interpretative remarks ("by far his most brilliant and impassioned plea for support"; his [the president's] lance pierced every weak spot in their [his opponents'] armor"; "this address stands out as the most notable he had made in the campaign"; and a less than entirely dispassionate evocation of the mood of the gathering ("roar after roar of approval seemed to upheave the great audience that filled Madison Square Garden to the last square inch"), constituted a bias in the president's favor, though, in the overall context of a report which accurately and fully reproduced much of the substance of the president's remarks, such bias was not serious. In all cases but one— the radio address to the *Herald Tribune* Forum, on 24 October 1940, the full text of the president's speech was carried by this newspaper.

Of the six reports in the *Washington Post*, five were fair and accurate and one was mildly biased in favor of the president. Reports were generally characterized by their fullness and by an absence of interpretative or evaluative comment. The report which was mildly biased in the president's favor added to these characteristics an insufficiently impartial description of the speech and its impact ("The president... smashed with verbal hammer blows [at the preceding administration]"; "...his entire audience seemed to sway expectantly under his feather-weight touches"). The texts of all six speeches were carried by the newspaper.

In its rigorous elimination of comment from its news columns and in its accurate, comprehensive, and impartial reporting of the subject matter of the president's six speeches, the *New York Times* was all but irreproachable, the only possible and very minor exception being a single comment in the report of the speech of 29 September 1936 ("Using every device of phrase and gesture in the manner he has mastered so well..."). All six speeches were reported fairly and ac-curately; in all cases, the texts of the speeches were reproduced.

Somewhat less exacting in their journalistic standards were the *New York Herald Tribune*, the *Washington Times Herald*, and the *New York Journal American*, although, in the latter two cases, as these two newspapers were not being published during the campaign of 1936, the sample of reports examined was small. Four of the *New York Herald Tribune*'s reports of Roosevelt's speeches were fair and accurate; two were biased against him, one mildly and one seriously. An otherwise comprehensive and balanced report of the speech of 11 September 1940, was flawed by the derogatory comment that Roosevelt "had not been above taking a political potshot at his Republican opponents" by repeating "the allegation of some of his New Deal 'hatchet men' that subsidiary companies of the power firm formerly headed by Mr. Willkie had hired 'labor spies,'" and by the possibly accurate but essentially speculative remark that the president's promise to improve and extend the old-age pension system constituted "a bid for the votes of Townsend old-age pension advocates." Additionally, serious bias was evident in the headlining of the president's Madison Square Garden speech of October 1936, which contained a hostile accusation ("Roosevelt Fails to Make Direct Reply to Rival"), and which generally highlighted the more provocative aspects of the president's remarks ("'Welcomes' Hatred of 'Forces' Opposing Him; Suggests Security Critics 'Emigrate'; Hopes 'Selfish' Foes with 'Lust for Power' Will Meet Their Master in His 2d Administration"). These exceptions aside, the reports of the *Herald Tribune* were characterized by a comprehensive and accurate coverage of the substance of the president's remarks. The texts of all six speeches were printed by this newspaper.

Generally, the accounts by the *Washington Times Herald* of the three speeches delivered during the presidential campaign of 1940 showed little distortion of the content of those speeches, although there was some evidence of a sympathetic attitude toward the president ("Boldly and eloquently, the president warned his radio audience..."; "There was a note of rugged, challenging confidence in his voice"). On balance, two of the speeches were reported fairly and accurately, and one, that of 12 October 1940, was reported in a manner which was slightly biased in the president's favor.

Treatment of the three speeches in the campaign of 1940 by the Hearst publication, the *New York Journal American*, varied. The important speech to the Teamsters' Union, on 11 September, was largely ignored, the newspaper making only indirect reference to it in an article on page five entitled "Willkie Hits Class Theory of Roosevelt."

Such treatment constituted serious bias against the president. Reporting of the speeches of 12 and 24 October, on the other hand, was full, adequate, and characterized by extensive quotation from the originals, although the practice of combining the headlines for separate articles on Willkie and the president tended to produce results unfavorable to the latter. Thus, in a report of the speech of 24 October, the headline: "Roosevelt Attacks Appeasers; Condemns 'Strategy of Terror,'" was intermingled with "Willkie Again Links Rival to Czech 'Deal'; Charges President Wired Hitler." On balance, however, the reporting of the two speeches of October 1940, was fair and accurate. The *Journal American* did not carry the texts of any of the president's speeches.

A relatively high degree of news distortion occurred in the remaining three newspapers. The report by the *New York World Telegram* of the speech delivered on 29 September 1936, was an accurate and straightforward account of the substance of the president's address and of the reaction to it. The text of this speech was carried by the newspaper. For the remainder, the speeches of 23 October 1936 and 11 September 1940, were reported fully and fairly, but were placed in inconspicuous positions in the *World Telegram*. The placement of the first report on page six of the newspaper revealed a mild bias against the president; the placing of the second on page ten of an issue which featured an attack on that speech ("Roosevelt Divided US Says Willkie; Asserts He Preaches Class Consciousness") on its front page indicated serious bias. The speeches of 12 and 24 October were not reported by the *World Telegram* and on the days on which such reports might have been anticipated, front-page stories which reflected unfavorably on the president appeared, the first entitled "Willkie Fears War by Roosevelt Slip: Says Blunder May Put U.S. in Unprepared," and the second "How about 4th Term, and 5th, Willkie Asks...." Serious bias occurred in both cases.

Of the six reports of Roosevelt's carried by the *Chicago Tribune*, three were seriously biased against the president, two were mildly biased, and one was fair and accurate. The account by the *Tribune* of Roosevelt's speech of 29 September 1936, which otherwise faithfully reproduced the contents of that address, quoting freely from the original, was flawed by the gratuitous comment that the president had

"ignored the charge of broken promises made against himself," and by
the assertion that his failure to release the text of the speech in time for
his opponents to formulate a reply on the same evening was "done on
the theory that the American people, if permitted to go to sleep after his
speech without listening to a reply, would not tune in on answers to
come." Notwithstanding these two statements, the degree of bias
against Roosevelt in this otherwise comprehensive report was considered to have been mild. Much more obvious was the bias in the
Tribune's reporting of the speeches of 23 and 31 October 1936. Although, in its acount of the former, the *Tribune* did print, verbatim, a
substantial portion of the president's remarks, the interpolation of a
sarcastic reference to the Good Neighbor League, which had sponsored
the talk, as "a 'nonpartisan' organization formed to cultivate the
church vote," and the gratuitous juxtaposition of the sentence "He
made no mention of the NRA" alongside a reported remark by
Roosevelt to the effect that the New Deal had taken a middle way in
order to "weld together the broken pipes of the circulatory system," at a
time when complete government control was being advocated by some,
constituted serious bias against the president. So far as the report of the
speech at Madison Square Garden, on 31 October 1936, was concerned, serious bias appeared in the *Tribune*'s headline ("Roosevelt
Talk Fails to Reply on NRA, AAA") and, equally obviously, in the
opening sentences of the report:

> In the supreme forensic effort of his campaign for reelection,
> President Roosevelt tonight failed to give a specific answer to the
> challenge of Governor Alf M. Landon that he declare his future
> objectives.
> He did not state definitly [sic] that he proposed to revive the un-
> constitutional agricultural adjustment act and the national recovery
> act if he is reelected. . . . He maintained silence. . .concerning the
> methods he will pursue to carry out his purposes.

The *Tribune* headlined its front-page account of the president's
speech of 11 September 1940, to the Teamsters' Union: "F.D.R. Urges
Labor to Keep Him in Power," and devoted a major section of what was
a relatively brief treatment of this wide-ranging and politically im-

portant address to a discussion of a controversy over the payment for the broadcasting of the speech, and, more specifically, over whether funding by the union of the broadcast would constitute a violation of the Hatch Act, which prohibited campaign contributions of more than $5,000 by any organization. Such treatment revealed serious bias against the president. Anti-Roosevelt bias in the *Tribune*'s report of the speech of 12 October 1940, was observable in the newspaper's assertion that, although the president had intended his address to be nonpolitical, it constituted "an answer to the charge of Wendell Willkie that the New Deal is seeking to bring the country into war," and in the observation that a tribute paid by the president to the Italian people of the Americas was "calculated to offset the deflection of votes among people of Italian blood who were angered by Mr. Roosevelt's phrase 'stab in the back' which he delivered in condemnation of Mussolini's entrance into the war." The report of the speech of 24 October was fair and accurate. The texts of the speeches of 29 September and 31 October 1936, and 11 September 1940, were reproduced by this newspaper; that of 12 October 1940, was partially reproduced.

The treatment by the *New York Sun* of the six presidential speeches was seriously biased against Roosevelt on five occasions and mildly biased against him on one. The gist of both the headlines and story-lead in the *Sun*'s report of the speech of 29 September 1936, was that Roosevelt had been forced, presumably unwillingly, to repudiate Communist support. Since, however, in the body of the report, the substance of the president's remarks was fully covered, only mild bias against the president occurred. Of the other speeches, three—those delivered on 23 October 1936, and 12 and 24 October 1940—were ignored by the *Sun*, treatment which clearly entailed serious bias against Roosevelt. The report of the speech of 11 September 1940, which, in itself, was a full and accurate account of the president's remarks, was carried on the seventh page of an issue which featured, on its front page, a story headed: "Willkie Calls Roosevelt Inept." Bias against Roosevelt was serious in this instance. Headed optimistically "President's Vague Appeal to Class Hatred Scares Nation as 45 Million Prepare to Vote," and positioned beneath banner headlines which proclaimed: "Landon Charges Revival of NRA Is Planned; Smith

Accuses Roosevelt of Bigoted Speech," the account of the remaining speech, the address at Madison Square Garden on 31 October 1936, dealt only briefly with the president's remarks, but discussed at some length what were said to be mass defections of voters to Landon. Thus, serious bias against Roosevelt again occurred. The text of only one speech, that of 29 September 1936, was reproduced by this newspaper.

The results of such an analysis suggest that, if the distortion of news by those publications which Roosevelt read each day was not widespread, neither was it uncommon, although, it is also clear, such a practice tended to be localized in some publications, rather than being characteristic of all.

A comparison between front-page reports of the press conferences which Roosevelt held at the White House during the three months preceding the 1936 and the 1940 elections with the transcripts of those press conferences, the results of which are shown in table 3, reveals relatively little direct evidence of distortion of news columns or of headlines.[19] Of 108 front-page articles examined in this way, only six were seriously biased against the president, and a further eight mildly biased against him. The remaining ninety-four reports were fair and accurate in their treatment of news emanating from Roosevelt's meetings with the Washington reporters.

Gradings given to the reports in three of the newspapers—the *Washington Post*, the *Chicago Tribune*, and the *New York Times*—accorded reasonably well with those made independently by another person. Variations in gradings occurred in relation to three of the seventeen reports by the *Washington Post*, and two of the five reports by the *Chicago Tribune*. With the *New York Times*, gradings failed to correspond for five of the nineteen stories, although, in the case of three of these, the discrepancies resulted from differences of opinion as to whether page-one reports had been based on material from press conferences or whether such material had been introduced, incidentally, into reports which were based substantially on other sources.[20]

Examination of the sample of front-page reports showed that, among the newspapers which the president read regularly, four—the *Washington Post*, the *New York Times*, the *New York Herald Tribune*, and the *Baltimore Sun*—gave extensive coverage to press conference announce-

Table 3: Front-Page Reporting of Roosevelt's White House Press Conferences by Nine Newspapers for Three-Month Period before 1936 and 1940 Elections*

Date of Press Conference	Newspapers								
1936	NYT	NYHT	CT	BS	WP	NYWT	NYS	NYJA	WTH
11 August	F	...	...	F	...	...	...		
25 August	F	F – M	F	– M	F	...	...		
8 September	...	...	– M	F	...	...	...		
11 September	...	...	...	...	...	...	...		
15 September	F F	F F	...	...	F	...	...		
6 October	F	...	...	F	F	...	...		
27 October	F	F F	...	F – M	F	...	...		
1940	NYT	NYHT	CT	BS	WP	NYWT	NYS	NYJA	WTH
2 August	F	F	– S	– M	F	F	F F	F	...
16 August	F	F	...	– S	F	F	F F	F	F
23 August	F	F	– S	F	F	F	F	F	F
27 August	F	F	...	– M	F	...	...	...	– M
6 September	...	...	...	...	F	...	F F	...	F
13 September	...	F	...	...	F	F	F F	...	...
24 September	...	...	...	...	...	...	...	...	...
27 September	F	...	...	...	...	...	...	...	...
1 October	...	F	...	F F	F	...	...	...	F F F
4 October	...	...	...	F	F	F	...	...	– S
4 October	F	...	– S	F	F	...	...	...	...
15 October	F F	F	...	F	...	...	...	...	– S
18 October	F	F	...	F	F	F	– M	...	F
22 October	F	...	...	...	F	...	...	...	...
25 October	F F	F	...	F	F	F	F	F	F
1 November	F	...	...	...	F	F	F	...	...

*NYT, New York Times; NYHT, New York Herald Tribune; CT, Chicago Tribune; BS, Baltimore Sun; WP, Washington Post; NYWT, New York World Telegram; NYS, New York Sun; NYJA, New York Journal American; WTH, Washington Times Herald; F, reporting fair and accurate; – M, reporting mildly biased against president; – S, reporting seriously biased against president; + M, reporting mildly biased in favor of the president; + S, reporting seriously biased in favor of the president; ellipses, no front-page report. (For any one date in any one newspaper, the number of symbols corresponds to the number of page-one stories based on a press conference.)

ments: the twenty-three press conferences in the sample gave rise to seventeen page-one reports in the *Post*, nineteen in the *Times*, fifteen in the *Herald Tribune*, and seventeen in the *Sun*. Treatment of news varied from newspaper to newspaper, but, generally, the reports in these publications showed minimal evidence of the distortion of which the president was prone to complain.

Without exception, the *Washington Post* reports were factual, accurate, and conspicuously free of tendentious or interpretative remarks. Evaluation of page-one articles in the *New York Times* proved to be more difficult. Written, for the most part, by the *Times'* Washington Bureau correspondent, Charles Hurd, the reports not infrequently went beyond a straightforward narrative of presidential announcements and press conference exchanges—though such were invariably included—to descriptions of the atmosphere of the press conferences and to observations derived inferentially from the president's answers or refusals to answer. On occasions, Hurd showed some animus against Roosevelt, usually prompted by the latter's failure to answer reporters' questions. Thus, for example, in his report of the press conference of 27 October 1936, Hurd observed: "About 100 newsmen laughed at the [president's] jokes but received few definite replies to inquiries." Nor did Hurd hesitate to make clear to readers the fact that the president was practicing evasion: when Roosevelt, quizzed at the same press conference about a remark alleged to have been made by his son, James, that the NRA would be revived during the next administration, refused to make a clear statement of his intentions, and referred the correspondents, instead, to his recent campaign speeches, Hurd commented: "So far as reporters could recall, the President has not mentioned the NRA in any of his speeches in this campaign." What followed, however, was an impeccably precise and correct account of other press conference questions and the president's responses to them. Not without some misgivings, it was decided that such reporting was fair and accurate, although it was appreciated that the president himself may not invariably have acquiesced in such a view.

The *New York Herald Tribune*, in its front-page reporting, reproduced the substance of the exchanges which took place at Roosevelt's press conferences with great fidelity. Fourteen of the fifteen reports examined were fair and accurate and one was mildly biased against the president. Only very occasionally were there interpolated into what were otherwise full and unadorned accounts of proceedings, comments of an interpretative or speculative nature. The newspaper's report of a press conference held on 25 August 1936, contained one example. Both Senator Carter Glass and the president at the press conference in question having remained tight-lipped about the matters discussed at a recent meeting, the *Herald Tribune* nevertheless dubbed the meeting a "peace conference," and asserted that Glass had received "reassuring promises of the White House course ahead on some subjects near to his heart." In the same report, the president's announcement of some relaxation in restrictions on PWA spending was interpreted by the newspaper as a gesture designed to pacify Secretary Ickes, who had been "smarting over a well-nigh complete blockade of his new P.W.A. program by White House regulations."

Of seventeen front-page reports in the *Baltimore Sun*, twelve were fair and accurate, four were mildly biased against the president, and one was seriously biased against him. Where it appeared, bias took the form of a disposition to emphasize inconsistencies in the policies of the administration, or in the statements of its supporters, or to include carping and gratuitous criticism in news reports. Thus, after the president had announced, at his press conference on 25 August 1936, a liberalization of crop-production loans, the *Sun's* report pointed out that this constituted a reversal of administration policy, the president having previously vetoed a crop-production loan bill which had passed both houses of Congress. Similarly, Roosevelt's evasiveness at his press conference on 27 October 1936, over the future of the NRA, led the *Sun's* correspondent to speculate, in relation to a forthcoming presidential trip, that that would be "one thing he will not touch upon." Nor did it seem essential for the *Sun* to take issue with the president's remark, made in the context of an explanation as to why he had not directly backed a conscription bill prior to doing so at his press conference of 2 August 1940, that he had ended the practice of sending ready-made bills to Congress and that none had gone up from him for a considerable time. "Apparently," observed the *Sun's* correspondent, "he overlooked the fact that his recommendation for executive power to call up the National Guard had been accompanied by a joint resolution giving effect to the message. That was less than a week ago."

Serious bias occurred in the *Sun*'s report of the press conference of 16 August 1940. In view of Roosevelt's repeated and explicit denials at this press conference that the transfer of destroyers to Britain was linked with negotiations for the acquisition of bases by the United States, both the headline of the report—"Roosevelt Willing to Swap Destroyers for Air-Sea Bases"—and the remainder of the *Sun*'s report ("The President issued a slightly cryptic and deliberately vague statement announcing that the conversations for such an arrangement are actually under way.") constituted a distortion of Roosevelt's remarks to reporters, if not of the agreement being formulated between the two countries.

At the other end of the spectrum is found the *Chicago Tribune*, in which the distortion of news columns appears to have been the norm. Of five front-page reports of Roosevelt's preelection press conferences, three were seriously biased against the president, and one mildly biased against him. It was characteristic of this newspaper to discuss presidential press conference announcements only in the context of anti-administration articles. Thus, Roosevelt's statement to reporters at a press conference on 8 September 1936, that the establishment of a "grid" system associated with the TVA was under discussion was linked by the *Tribune* with a story of a "row" between representatives of the New Deal and executives of the country's gas and electric utilities. The dispute was said to have "stirred" Italian delegates to the current world power conference, leading these representatives to assert that even the Fascist state still welcomed private ownership and operation of utilities. A "grid" system, the *Tribune*'s report asserted, "involves the first step leading to government control of all utilities." A further example of this technique occurred in the *Tribune*'s reporting of the president's press conference on 2 August 1940. Having been asked, at that conference, to comment on a reported feeling in congressional circles that he was "not very hot" about conscription proposals then before Congress, Roosevelt repudiated the suggestion and took the unusual step of permitting direct quotation of his remarks to reporters to the effect that he was "distinctly in favor of a selective service bill" and "consider[ed] it essential to adequate national defense." The *Tribune* reported the president's remarks in a story headlined "Draft Plan Hit by Woodring.... Warns of Perils in Compulsory Law," which gave much greater prominence to a statement by former secretary of war, Harry H. Woodring, condemning the administration's conscription program as "a step toward totalitarianism." The article went on to suggest that Woodring's statement "proved the contention of opponents of the [conscription] legislation that the army was against it."

Serious bias against Roosevelt was evident, also, in the reporting of an exchange which took place in his press conference of 8 October 1940, concerning his recent consultations with Admiral Richardson and Admiral Leahy. In answer to repeated queries as to the relationship between these conversations and the current crisis in the Far East, the president would say only that the conferees had been "just studying maps." This exchange between the president and newsmen was reported by the *Tribune* in the context of an article which suggested that "New Dealers," by pressing forward with warlike preparation, were moving to foment a crisis with Japan in order to obviate the danger of a two-ocean attack on the United States in the future.

For the remainder of the newspapers which Roosevelt read each day, the *New York World Telegram* carried eight front-page reports based on Roosevelt's press conferences, and, without exception, such reports were fair and accurate and free of any attempt to present news in a manner which reflected unfavorably on the president. However, its reporting of White House news may not have been representative of this newspaper's journalistic standards, since all the reports in question came from the United Press, one of the national news associations. Similarly, the four front-page stories based on Roosevelt's press conferences carried by the *New York Journal American* were obtained through the International News Services, and their fairness and accuracy could not, in these instances at least, be faulted.

The *New York Sun*, which maintained strong editorial opposition to New Deal policies, reported the president's press conferences in considerable detail and with great fidelity, a total of eleven out of twelve front-page stories on the president's preelection press conferences having been fair and accurate. Mild bias did occur in a front-page report of 18 October 1940, which dealt with Roosevelt's announcement that he intended to enter the election campaign to counter the campaign of deliberate falsification being waged by his opponents. Animus against the president appeared in the *Sun*'s correspondent's reference to the disappearance of the "atmosphere of cocksure confidence" which had marked recent press conferences, in the statement that Roosevelt, "always the showman," had "continued to cultivate carefully the appealing grin which is so characteristic of him" and in the interpretation of the president's remarks as a politically motivated attack on the Republican nominee, Willkie, whom the president, in his statement, did not name.

Of eleven front-page stories in the *Washington Times Herald* based on White House press conferences in the period before the 1940 election, two were seriously biased against the president and one mildly biased against him. A full and substantially accurate account of the important press conference held on 27 August 1940, was flawed by a gratuitous reference to Roosevelt as the "famed nemesis of big business," and by the assertion that he had entered the controversy over the nation's preparedness program "with bitter relish." More obvious was the bias in the *Times Herald*'s report of the press conference on 4 October 1940, at which Roosevelt, on being asked by a reporter whether he had any reason to believe that Germany and Italy were working for his defeat in the coming election, answered by reading to the reporters a dispatch from a special correspondent, which asserted that this was so. He refused to comment further on the matter. Under the circumstances, the *Times Herald*'s headline: "Axis Seeks His Defeat, Roosevelt Declares," and the story-lead: "President Roosevelt told the American people in effect yesterday that any voter who casts a ballot against his 3rd term follows the wishes of Hitler and Mussolini," were hardly justified.

The other instance of serious distortion occurred in the reporting of the press conference of 15 October 1940, at which the president announced that he had issued an executive order authorizing the export of arms, machine tools, and other articles, the purchase of which, by other countries, had previously been forbidden under the Neutrality and Export Control Acts. Asked by a reporter whether the order had any connection with current conversations with Russia on the release of machine tools, the president replied: "I suppose so—yes; probably the same thing." Asked, again, whether machine tools would be available for Russia, Roosevelt replied: "In other words, the general idea is, if we don't need them for ourselves we turn them over to a friendly power." The exchange continued:

> Q: And Russia is a friendly power?
> The President: I don't think Russia is the mainspring in that.
> Q: Just incidental?
> The President: Yes.

Under the circumstances, the *Time Herald*'s headline: "Soviet to Get Needed Tools from U.S.: F.D. Wooing Stalin from Axis; Calls Russia 'Friendly,'" and two statements in the body of the report—"Going out of his way to characterize the Soviet Union as a 'friendly power,'" and "[The President] eagerly agreed Russia was 'a friendly power'"—were a perversion of the letter and spirit of the president's remarks.

Typically, however, where bias in the treatment of news emanating from Roosevelt's press conferences occurred, it consisted not so much in the unfair reporting and presentation of such news, as in the failure to report it at all. In this respect, variations in their treatment of presidential press conference news among the newspapers whose front-page reporting has been sampled are striking and eloquent. Out of twenty-three press conferences held over the periods examined, the *Chicago Tribune* found material for only five front-page stories (which, in any case, were not based wholly, or even mainly, on press conference material), as against nineteen for the *New York Times*, seventeen for the *Baltimore Sun* and the *Washington Post*, and fifteen for the *New York Herald Tribune*. From sixteen press conferences held in the three-month period before the 1940 election, the Hearst *New York Journal American* derived but four front-page stories. While it is impossible to draw conclusions from a newspaper's treatment of material provided from any one, or even a small number, of press conferences, the persistent failure by a given publication to carry important presidential news on its front pages can hardly be attributed to inadvertence or to occasional idiosyncratic judgment of relative news values. On these grounds, charges of bias apply also, though with less force, to the *New York Sun* and the *New York World Telegram*, which drew no material for page-one stories from the president's press conferences before the 1936 election and from, in both cases, eight of the sixteen conferences held in the period before the 1940 elections.

On 18 October 1942, the *Louisville Courier Journal* took Franklin Roosevelt to task for his criticisms of the American press. Quoting a recent remark by Walter Lippmann that "he [Roosevelt] is so much annoyed with so many of us that his displeasure, like the rain, falls equally upon the just and the unjust," the newspaper's editorial writer proceeded to discuss possible reasons for the president's hostility. Foremost among these, he suggested, was not the memory of Roosevelt's past treatment by the press, although this had been, by certain newspapers, and particularly during the campaign of 1936, blatantly unfair; but, rather, the restricted nature of the president's knowledge of the content of the nation's newspapers. "He probably doesn't know," the editorial writer surmised, "what newspapers outside of Washington, Baltimore, New York and Chicago, are saying or doing." Ignorant of the patriotic support which the press of America was giving to the war effort, unmindful of the fact that "there never was as small a segment of it [the press] 'riding' him as there is today," the president was erroneously judging all sections of the press by its most partisan and disreputable units. "We suspect," the *Courier Journal* stated, "it is not his long memory so much as his daily reading fare that keeps him irritated these days."

What the analyses of the reporting of the president's speeches and press conferences by the newspapers which he read each day suggest, however, is that, even in relation to his "daily reading fare," Roosevelt's charges of widespread and persistent distortion of news could not fairly have been sustained. What these analyses indicate, rather, is that the reporting of news emanating from the president's press conferences was fair and accurate in the vast majority of cases, that the reporting of the president's speeches was fair and accurate in a majority of cases, and that, where bias did occur, it tended to be localized in certain newspapers, rather than being characteristic of most.

The issue of the extent to which Roosevelt's assertion that story slanting was characteristic of the press was borne out by the evidence of which he was aware is not as clear-cut as was the question of whether Roosevelt exaggerated the extent of editorial opposition to his policies. Complaints received by the White House about the handling of news by Hearst and McCormick publications, and about the lack of patriotic commitment on the part of certain newspapers during the war, were numerous; distorted reporting of the president's speeches by certain newspapers was not infrequent. Yet, notwithstanding such considerations, there remains a gap between Roosevelt's generalized statements about owner-inspired story slanting and the actual journalistic practices of those sections of the press of which he had direct and reliable knowledge, and, in relation to this issue, as with the question of the extent of press opposition which he faced, it appears probable that Franklin Roosevelt, who so strenuously objected to the distortion of news, was himself distorting the record.

Nothing Would Help Him More than to Have It Known That the Newspapers Were All against Him

To contemporaries, the notion that Franklin Roosevelt possessed, toward the American press as a whole, a deep-seated antagonism was something of a commonplace. At times, the strength of that antagonism perturbed the president's supporters. Roy Howard called Roosevelt's attention, in August 1935, to a growing public awareness of his hostility toward the press, and, criticizing his practice of attributing the faults of the few to the many, suggested that the president might take occasion to "re-emphasize his appreciation that all American journalism is not to be judged on the basis of its most partisan units." But his suggestion went unheeded.[r] Raymond Moley expressed similar misgivings. Having previously noted a tendency on the part of Roosevelt to comment angrily on newspaper articles and to show a perverse interest in stories critical of himself, Moley became perturbed, in April 1936, over Roosevelt's apparent determination to attack the press, and, Moley thought, needlessly to provoke its hatred.[2] William Allen White was another to manifest concern over the president's growing offense at that institution. Speaking for the American Newspaper Publishers' Association at its annual press conference at the White House in April 1939, White was conciliatory: "Most of us," he told Roosevelt, "have agreed with most of the things that you have tried to do. If some of us have disagreed with a few of the things, it was in sorrow, not in anger, and it hurt us much more than it did you. (Laughter)." Some months later, White wrote to urge the president not to let the newspapers "get in your hair." "They do the best they can do," said he, "and you do the best you can do and in both cases it is a pretty good job."[3]

Charges that Roosevelt was unreasonably hostile toward the newspapers of America were frequently aired in the press itself. A *Kiplinger Washington Letter* published early in Roosevelt's second term, referred to his "growing irritation at the press" and his constant criticism of its proprietors. Franklin Waltman, writing in the *Washington Post* of 1 July 1937, alluded to the "increasing contempt for the press" displayed by the White House since the recent election and lamented that "at virtually every press conference, the President makes some sally at the press." Roosevelt's "deepening offense" at the press, declared a *Kiplinger Washington Letter*, in April 1938, "is a situation of public importance." [4]

Such criticisms were to continue. As reported by the *New York Times* of 8 October 1940, Arthur Krock, in a recent address to the New York State Society of Newspaper Editors, had drawn attention to the constant attempt, on the part of the administration, "to preach a class war against the press," while from the president himself, Krock charged, had come "steady implications that the press is unreliable and often venal." Returning to his theme in his column in the *New York Times* of 22 February 1941, Krock declared that "the President and his chief aides have lost few opportunities to weaken public faith in the integrity of the news columns."

The record of Roosevelt's conversations with the Washington reporters is similarly eloquent on this point: Roosevelt rarely mentioned the press except to criticize it, and his criticisms were a recurring theme.

Hostility was evidenced, too, not only in Roosevelt's general reluctance to praise the press, but in his particular inability to do so unambiguously. In his radio address to the *New York Herald Tribune* Forum on 26 October 1939, he did pay an uncharacteristic tribute to "the majority of the press" because, during the critical international situation of the previous weeks, it had "tried to discriminate between fact and propaganda and unfounded rumor, and to give...readers... an unbiased and factual chronicle of developments." But he could not then resist adding that "this has worked so well in international reporting that one may be pardoned for wishing for more of it in the field of domestic news." [5] The same inhibition was shown yet more clearly in Roosevelt's tenth fireside chat of October 1937, in which he discussed the way in which the public was being educated about their government. "Five years of fierce discussion and debate, five years of information through the radio and the moving picture," the president declared, "have taken the whole nation to school in the nation's business." The omission was noted. "It is typical of him," wrote columnist Frank R. Kent, "that he should try to disparage the press by the sly intimation that it does not educate the people, while the radio and the moving pictures do." [6]

The idea that Franklin Roosevelt possessed a settled and deep-seated aversion toward the press is suggested by and consistent with certain of the results of this study, which reveal, on his part, a disposition to magnify the faults of the press and to depict it in highly unfavorable terms. Thus, investigation of the editorial treatment of the Roosevelt administration by the American press has demonstrated not merely that Roosevelt's assertion that the overwhelming majority, or 85 percent, of the press opposed him was an exaggeration in fact, but that it was hardly compatible with the record of press treatment of his administration which was revealed either through his own daily newspaper reading or through the reports reaching him from the Division of Press Intelligence. Similarly, evidence concerning the coloration of news, which reached Roosevelt, should have indicated that the practice of "story slanting" by the press, though by no means rare, tended to be localized, rather than endemic. Significant also, in this regard, is the suggestion that Franklin Roosevelt exaggerated the extent of the opposition of newspaper owners, and the recognition that his blanket condemnations of newspaper owners as a class are not easily reconciled with his relations with members of that group as individuals.

Deep-seated hostility is suggested, also, by the extreme inflexibility of Roosevelt's views, by his reluctance to acknowledge press support where it existed, and by his indifference to it where it was offered. Nothing could shift him from his beliefs that the overwhelming majority of the press was against him, and that reporters were under orders to slant their dispatches against his administration, assertions which he continued to make without apparent regard to changes in his relations with newspaper publishers as individuals, or shifts in the known level of his press support. He enjoyed, though he did not acknowledge, the general backing of the southern and Negro presses;[7] the support which he received from weekly publications was consistently above that given by the country's daily newspapers;[8] but these obvious advantages brought from him no favorable or appreciative comment. Indeed, there is a suggestion that when, early in his second term, the president's attack on the Supreme Court, and the administration's increasingly anti-Fascist stand induced the leading liberal journals to throw their weight behind the New Deal, Roosevelt treated their friendly overtures with indifference.[9]

Nor did what the press saw as an increasing measure of support for the administration's foreign policies and its patriotic assistance to the war effort cause any apparent abatement in Roosevelt's resentment, or any modification of his views. From well before the outbreak of war, Division of Press Intelligence reports must have shown Roosevelt that his foreign policies were receiving substantial backing from the press. Yet despite such cooperation, which continued to be revealed by such surveys, by the attitudes expressed to Roosevelt by representatives of the business press, at their annual meetings with him, and, later, by the success of the voluntary censorship system, Roosevelt's attacks continued. Protest was frequent. When the president berated the press, at his conference with reporters on 21 February 1941, for publishing statements made by General George C. Marshall to the Senate Military Affairs Committee, and "leaked" by members of that committee to reporters, columnist Raymond Clapper took him to task for his ingratitude: the president's attack, Clapper complained, had coincided with the release by the British Embassy of directly parallel information, and had occurred, moreover, at a time when the publishers had made a patriotic approach to the government to offer their assistance in the defense effort. Clapper continued:

> The newspaper world is responding as it has not responded in the last eight years to Mr. Roosevelt's leadership. Yet the press as a whole now has its morals and patriotism hauled into question for a decision of judgment although it made the same decision that the British embassy made with regard to parallel information.[10]

Clapper's complaint was echoed by *Editor and Publisher* on 17 October 1942:

The persistent hectoring and sneering at newspapermen by the President is not deserved. . . . The newspapers are doing a valiant and effective job of forwarding the war effort. . . . Recognition of that fact by the President in his public addresses would be far more appropriate than the sneers which so often mark his public references to newspapers and their ownership and direction.

Roosevelt's disposition to minimize press support where it existed was vividly illustrated toward the end of 1944, when he was asked to sign a batch of letters to newspapers which had backed him in the recent campaign. Publications to be favored in such a manner had been selected with great care. Instead of relying on the survey of political allegiances conducted by *Editor and Publisher*, Paul A. Porter, director of publicity for the Democratic National Committee, had telegraphed state Democratic chairmen to obtain the names of local newspapers which had fought for Roosevelt. To these had been added those publications, listed by *Editor and Publisher* as supporting the president, whose actual allegiance to him the Division of Press Intelligence had been able to confirm after "culling hundreds of . . . clippings." As the division had been able to check only a small fraction of the pro-Roosevelt newspapers on *Editor and Publisher*'s list (because it subscribed to only a limited number of them), and as, where it had been so checked, that magazine's list had proved to be "one hundred percent correct," the list of newspapers which it submitted to the president, the Democratic National Committee pointed out to him, substantially understated the level of his newspaper support.

Under the circumstances, Roosevelt's reaction, on being asked to sign the first batch of letters of appreciation, is interesting: he objected that the number was too great, refused absolutely to sign a letter to the president of the *Macon News and Telegraph*, and expressed reservations about signing several other letters because the newspapers concerned "had been too bitter against the Administration." He then stated "very decisively" to Presidential Secretary William Hassett that he would sign no more letters, and instructed Stephen Early to reexamine those which he had signed with a view to eliminating those to publications which had been too hostile.[11] The scrutiny of the nation's press by the Democratic National Committee and the Division of Press

Intelligence had been meticulous, but, clearly, the president's own standards were more exacting.

At his annual press conference with newspaper editors in April 1939, Roosevelt read to the group one of a number of questions submitted to him beforehand by the editors. "Is your seeming dislike of the American press..." one questioner had begun. "There ain't any," interposed Roosevelt. "He starts wrong, I love it." Conceivably, few of them would have believed him.

The reasons for Franklin Roosevelt's apparently unyielding hostility toward the press were the subject of recurrent speculation by contemporaries. Complaining, editorially, on 1 July 1943, that it was "not a dignified spectacle to see the President use his press conference time after time as a vehicle for flaying the free press of America," the *Washington Post*, in attempting an explanation of his latest onslaught, speculated that it might have been attributable to the anger of a man who, embarrassed by the shortcomings of his administration, was using the press as a "whipping boy." Alternatively, Robert L. Riggs, writing in the *Louisville Courier-Journal* of 11 October 1942, wondered whether the president's practice of "needling the press" may have had, for him, a therapeutic function, affording the chief executive both a method of relaxation and far greater pleasure than his other major hobby of collecting stamps.

Such explanations aside, it is clear that Roosevelt sometimes projected onto the press the hostility of a determined politician thwarted in some of his cherished schemes. Angered by the opposition of certain sections of the northern press to his attempt, in 1938, to purge "reactionary" elements in his own party, he directed Thomas Corcoran to have "some well-known personality in Georgia, like the President of a University," attack such publications in a radio address. Newspapers advocating the reelection of Senator George were to be singled out for special attention. The *Boston Herald* should, said Roosevelt, be characterized as "one paper above all in the United States representative of the old-fashioned New England abolitionist thought"; the *New York Herald-Tribune* as "the paper which represents the great absentee landlords who draw from the South the tribute which keeps the South poor." Roosevelt's memorandum continued:

Go through the list across the country, through the Chicago
Tribune to the Los Angeles Times.

You Southerners, how do you like that—your enemies in the
North...are praying for the reelection of Senator George.

Don't you sense the implications for all that Southerners are and
believe in the support of Senator George by the abolitionists and
absentee Northern landlord [sic].[12]

Through this memorandum, Roosevelt was obviously seeking to counter
hostile newspaper comment; he was also displaying a bitterness that is
startling, projecting his own frustrations and resentments, and attempting to project those of the South, onto certain sections of the
northern press which were opposing his "reforms."

More generally, the opposition of a substantial segment of the press
to the New Deal would have aroused the president's enmity. On a
straight, quantitative basis that opposition may have been much less
than Roosevelt claimed, but its often violent and personally abusive
tone could have evoked, on his part, overreaction and exaggeration,
with his legitimate hostility to some sections of the press carelessly
spilling over into more comprehensive indictments. Examples of such
abusive press comment abound. There were, for example, attacks on
the president's family, including, in 1938, a spate of criticism concerning the activities of his sons. "Sixteen times since March 26, 1933,"
trumpeted the Los Angeles Times one year later, "the three sons of the
President of the United States have made the front pages of the
country's press for the manner in which they drive their automobiles."
There was the distilled bitterness of Westbrook Pegler, who, in a
comment on a statement by the president's wife, in support of national
service, that "there would be the advantage that young men from all
the different groups which make up the citizenship of the nation, would
be thrown together," noted, in the Washington Times Herald of 24
October 1944 that "neither Mrs. Roosevelt nor her husband have [sic]
set foot in a public school and, when she had young ones, she saw to it
that neither did they." In his column of the following day Pegler
returned to the attack: "Some readers of these dispatches have asked
why I recently exposed the participation of the late Warren Delano, the
President's grandfather, in the infamous opium smuggling trade, one

of the sources of the Roosevelt family fortune." Enlightenment followed: "Franklin D. Roosevelt and his wife have lived all their lives in extravagant luxury and snobbery on vile and guilty gains whose source they could not but have known."

There may also have been, in Franklin Roosevelt's comprehensive assaults on the press, a degree of political calculation that was at once more rational and more purposeful. His exaggeration of the amount of press opposition, his apparent overestimation of the extent to which distortion of news occurred, and the general inflexibility of his views in the face of evidence which might have been expected to modify them, would then be interpreted as part of an attempt which aimed, by painting the press in the worst possible colors, to put that institution on the defensive, to encourage introspection or timidity, and to blunt, thereby, the sharp and politically disconcerting edge of its criticism. If not precise calculation, political intuition might have convinced Roosevelt of the effectiveness of such a course.

It is unnecessary to deny the importance of such factors in order to appreciate that, as a close examination of his critique of that institution shows, Roosevelt's resentment against the press was both related to, and rationalized in terms of, his own conception of its necessary role in the democratic system, and its failure, in his eyes, adequately to fulfill that role. Recognition of this fact throws revealing light not merely on the origin of Roosevelt's antagonism but also on the nature which, characteristically, it assumed.

The press's essential task, Roosevelt believed, was to act as a channel through which the best available information could flow from a preeminently well-informed government to an intelligent and democratically minded people. In a letter on the subject of "a free press" to Frank D. Schroth, editor of the *Brooklyn Daily Eagle*, Roosevelt referred, by implication, to that role:

> These times...demand above all else truth in the news, for it is corollary of our democracy that the public can be depended upon to assess problems and policies at their true value if facts are presented as facts, and opinion as opinion.[13]

That he saw the government itself as the major source of such information (and the press as sometimes failing to transmit it to the people) was clear from remarks he made in a radio interview in May 1939. Announcing the inauguration of a series of nationwide radio reports by members of the cabinet, aimed, among other things, at answering questions from the public on the work of their departments, Roosevelt declared:

> I like the idea of keeping the broadcasts entirely factual. . . . It should be possible. . . through. . . [these] broadcasts, to correct the kind of misinformation that is sometimes given currency. . . . In some communities it is the unhappy fact that only through the radio, is it possible to overtake loudly proclaimed untruths or greatly exaggerated half truths. . . . *They* [the people] *have a right to expect their Government to keep them supplied with the sober facts in every possible way* [italics mine].[14]

Certain characteristic features of the Roosevelt critique of the press are consonant with this view of the press's necessary function within the democratic system. This is particularly true of the president's attitude toward "interpretation." Roosevelt's repeated strictures against this practice amounted to something more than the customary insistence on the separation of news and comment. To an extent, he was objecting, also, to what he correctly perceived to be a new development in the treatment of news, a change which reporters also recognized, though they did not equally deplore. Looking back, some correspondents were able to fix the day in 1933 on which the United States abandoned the gold standard as the precise point at which the old journalism failed, for, having tried unsuccessfully to report intelligibly on that event, they had been forced to appeal to the White House for assistance and were provided with a government economist to help them prepare their dispatches. Increasingly confronted, from that time, with a growing complexity of events, reporters felt the need to explain and to clarify the matters about which they wrote, rather than merely to transmit a record of them to their readers—which is precisely why Roosevelt's long "background" discussions at his press conference were so greatly appreciated by them.[15] But Roosevelt could never accept the legitimacy of such interpretative efforts.

He could not do so because he believed that, by embellishing pure "facts" with extraneous comment, those within the press who interpreted were impeding the free and necessary flow of information from government to people, and threatening, in this way, to break a vitally important informational circuit in the democratic system. At best, interpretation was unnecessary, since the people were capable of understanding the complex affairs of government, provided they were given the necessary facts. "Mr. President," a reporter asked Roosevelt at a press conference on 7 November 1934, "do you think the ordinary...the intelligent reader of a newspaper is in a position to...judge from a bare presentation of the facts?" "Pretty close to it," he replied, "yes." At worst, interpretation was corrosive, serving to destroy the people's faith in the press itself. But Roosevelt's objection to interpretation ran well beyond his obvious fear that, because of it, the channels of national communication would become muddied. What he clearly believed, also, was that all attempts, other than his own, to interpret national events were misguided and inadequate, because his rivals in this field lacked his sources of information and his breadth of vision. Thus, while, in theory, attempts by newspaper editors to discuss the nation's affairs were legitimate, in practice, the efforts of such petty interpreters could hardly succeed. In his annual conference with newspaper editors in April 1938, Roosevelt reminded his listeners of their inferiority: "I am more closely in touch with public opinion... than any individual in this room.... You...cannot get a national picture the way I can." In the same conference he remarked patronizingly that, though Washington reporters tried "awfully hard," and were "a grand crowd," not one of them could understand "the ramifications of the national problems." At an earlier press conference with the editors of trade papers, on 14 February 1936, he had sympathized with those present for "having to write editorials on more than you know," on topics which, said he, "I couldn't write on myself, knowing three times as many facts as you do"; and in a scornful reaction to editorial comment on his Quarantine Speech he told the Washington corps on 6 October 1937, that "there are no two of them that agree," and that "most [editorial writers] cannot visualize the thing at all."

In Roosevelt's detestation of newspaper columnists his hatred of interpretation reached its peak. Even the most respected among them were obviously deficient. "In spite of his brilliance," he said of Walter

Lippmann on one occasion, "it is very clear that he has never let his mind travel west of the Hudson or north of the Harlem!"[16] Not only did columnists encourage, in reporters, the tendency to interpret, but, quintessentially, they were, themselves, interpreters, presumptuous and manifestly incompetent rivals, who challenged his own rightful preeminence as the legitimate interpreter of the affairs of the nation.

Roosevelt's views were sharply challenged. The Washington reporters were never prepared to accept that his "interpretations" and "the facts" were one and the same thing, to act as ciphers, to acquiesce in a view of their functions which would have had the effect of preventing the release not merely of imperfect, but of politically embarrassing information. Yet the president continued to urge this role on them, and to dismiss scornfully those who more directly sought to comment, through the press, on the affairs of the nation.

Roosevelt's comprehensive criticisms of interpretation were reiterated with a confidence which can scarcely have been based on the logic of his position, and, while it is appreciated that acceptance by the press of his notions that, where interpretation was required, he was most capable of supplying it, and that none but his own interpretations were to be regarded as "facts" worthy of being reported, would have been to his political advantage, both his dogmatism and his inconsistency suggest that, to him, a belief in the impropriety of "interpretation" may have been not merely politically expedient, but axiomatic.

Also consonant with his belief in the importance of straight, factual reporting were Roosevelt's determination to scrutinize the press closely and to correct inaccuracies in news reports where these occurred.

Roosevelt's close surveillance of the press predated the presidential period. In the 1920s he subscribed to several press-clipping services, and, as governor of New York, he made a daily study of a considerable quantity of news clippings and editorials relating to his own policies and performance.[17] Where he was dissatisfied, he either sent, or had his associates send, letters of complaint to the editors of offending publications.

Sometimes, such letters had an obviously important political purpose. Thus, for example, in June 1929, Roosevelt wrote with understandable concern to the editor of the *Elmira* (New York) *Advertiser*, protesting about a statement that he was "an exceedingly tired man," and that the governorship was proving "a severe tax upon his strength, for he is by no means well." Later that year he instructed his secretary to "get local people to write letters to the Republican papers which are getting out deliberately false statements"; and in April 1930, he himself wrote to the editor of the *Lowville* (New York) *Democrat* asking for authentication of the statement that, just after the 1928 election, he (Roosevelt) had "declared that Al Smith had been 'cheated' out of the presidency."[18] On other occasions, however, Roosevelt's objections were trifling. Special Assistant Samuel Rosenman was surprised when Roosevelt, who was resting at Warm Springs after the 1930 legislative session, arranged to have many editorials and news items clipped and sent to him, and then "busily singled out those that were unfavorable...and was ready to go to no end of trouble to correct any misunderstanding or error of fact." Roosevelt, Rosenman has recalled, "did this constantly—sometimes about subjects that seemed to me quite trivial, and often with very unimportant newspapers." One example mentioned by the governor's assistant concerned an editorial in the *Binghamton Press*, which had asserted that one effect of a proposed piece of legislation would be to create an open season for grouse that year. Roosevelt requested Rosenman to have Conservation Commissioner Alec Macdonald write to the newspaper repudiating this suggestion, and expressing indignation at the thought that the Conservation Department would "encourage the extinction of ruffed grouse."[19]

In January 1931, a letter which, though not signed by Roosevelt, bore, nevertheless, the unmistakable stamp of his style, attacked the editor of the *Chicago Post* over an editorial on the recent inauguration ceremony. The editorial had stated that, although "preparations had been made for a great outpouring of people," the expected delegations "did not materialize; the amplifiers were not used; the assembly chamber was 'half empty.'" Having branded these statements "completely false," Roosevelt went on to present "the simple facts": the inaugural ceremonies had been kept as simple as possible, the cost having been reduced from $21,000 to $3,500; no guests from other states had been been invited, except "about fifteen personal friends of the Governor's"; far from being "half empty," the Senate Chamber had been "more than filled," since, although there were twenty-five vacant seats in the corner of one gallery, three or four hundred people had been standing at the rear of the chamber.[20] Though it represented a legitimate complaint, Roosevelt's letter was an absolute triumph of pedantry.

Although the volume of such letters decreased sharply after he became president, Franklin Roosevelt's close scrutiny of the press continued. An indefatigable reader and critic of newspapers, Roosevelt punctuated his press conferences with comments on the performance of the press which revealed, on his part, a surprisingly detailed knowledge of newspaper content. His claim, at a press conference on 15 April 1937, that he had checked the content of "gossip columns" for a month and had discovered that the percentage of "absolute manufactured error" was as high as 40 percent, was scarcely believable, but was nevertheless indicative of his disposition to monitor the press, and of his continuing, and, at times, almost passionate concern for its accuracy. So, also, was his practice of summoning offending editors to the White House and requiring them to explain inconsistencies and inaccuracies in their publications. In September 1942, for example, Roosevelt called Edwin L. James, managing editor of the *New York Times*, to the White House to discuss editorial inconsistencies in the *Times* over the preceding two months. In February 1943, the editor of *PM* received a similar summons.[21]

What seemed, at times, to amount almost to a fetishism by Roosevelt for straight, factual, even literal reporting was illustrated most graphically in a letter which he wrote to Henry Luce in November 1940. The subject of the letter was an article in *Time* which had described election night at Roosevelt's Hyde Park residence. The article, Roosevelt declared, was "written with such a complete disregard of the facts" that he felt that he must use it as an example. Confining his attention to the first column of the story, Roosevelt then began a sentence-by-sentence analysis of the offending piece. The second and third sentences of the second paragraph read:

Hyde Park House was dark, the big green shutters swung snug to the front windows—from outside, not a crack of light showed from the library. Inside and out, the atmosphere was solemn, expectant, tense.

This sentence [*sic*], Roosevelt complained,

> gives, of course, the impression that conditions in the Hyde Park House were different from usual. The shutters are, of course, always closed and the house is dark from the outside. The atmosphere inside was not solemn, and not tense. The adjectives are just the opposite of the truth. The adjective "expectant" was, of course, correct.

The first sentence in the second paragraph of the article read:

> In station wagons and long shining limousines came people in evening clothes, neighbors and friends.

That sentence, complained Roosevelt,

> gives the impression that the people who came to the house were in evening clothes. A rather careful check shows that about ten per cent were in evening clothes. . . .

Paragraph three had begun:

> Apart from his household, alone at the mahogany table in the family dining room, sat the master mathematician of U.S. politics. Outside the room's closed doors was expectant silence.

In his letter, Roosevelt referred to the first sentence of this paragraph as a "deliberate falsehood"; he had been in the family dining room but "people in the 'household' were drifting in and out all the time." The second sentence contained "a double lie"; the only one of five doors to the room that had been closed was the one leading to the hall and this had been closed to keep out the draft from the front door.

At the conclusion of a long and detailed critique, the president explained his major concern. Those who had firsthand knowledge of the events on which *Time* reported would, after reading those reports, conclude that they were "based on deliberate misrepresentation instead of on facts." Gradually, increasing numbers of people would come to realize that they could not trust what they read. The article, he concluded, was typical of "a form of journalism which your President is perfectly willing to tell you he thinks of serious detriment to the future of successful democracy in the United States."[22]

Even allowing for *Time*'s past journalistic misdemeanors, for the

generally hostile attitude of that magazine and its publisher toward the
president, and for the accumulated resentment to which these may
have given rise, Roosevelt's attack was curious. The offending story
had been based on the reporting of Felix Belair, who had been outside
the Hyde Park house on election night and had interviewed a number
of people who had been inside the house when the election returns
came in.[23] Given that inaccuracies had occurred, they concerned matters which seemed trivial and politically innocuous, and, in relation to
which, expressions such as "deliberate falsehood," "double lie,"
"wholly false," and "deliberate misrepresentation" hardly seemed
appropriate, or in any way proportionate to the nature of the supposed
offense. Nor had the story reflected any discredit on the president. The
explanation as to why Roosevelt, in the full flush of his third-term
victory, and in a period of grave international crisis should have taken
time to compose such a letter is not immediately apparent, unless,
perhaps, one is to credit his assertion that, as a result of this and
similar articles, the foundations of American democratic society might
crumble.

Seen in the context of Roosevelt's general critique of the American
press, however, the letter to Luce is less peculiar, reflecting, as it does,
Roosevelt's apparently obsessional concern over what the press was
saying, no matter on how unimportant a subject; reflecting, also, his
insistence on factual, even literal reporting, his assumption that, where
mistakes occurred, they were never inadvertent, but representative of a
settled policy on the part of the publication involved, and a conception
of the role of the press which not only ruled out what to others seemed a
modicum of harmless speculation, but saw such practices as constituting a threat to democracy itself.

Franklin Roosevelt's controlling ideas about and distinctive attitudes
toward the press may be thrown into sharper relief if they are set
alongside those of the other major administration spokesman on press
matters—Harold Ickes. Himself the target of much unfavorable press
comment, Ickes set down his views about that institution in an extended series of public criticisms which he undertook with characteristic vigor and sustained with typical polemical ability.

Like Roosevelt, Ickes was concerned to stress the weight of press opposition with which the administration was saddled, and the discrepancy between it and the level of popular support. Like Roosevelt, too, the Secretary of the Interior professed to believe that an increasingly intelligent public was becoming more and more critical of the press and drawing conclusions that would embarrass certain publishers "if they could only lift their eyes higher than the safes in their counting rooms." Moreover, Ickes' description of a statement by the *Wall Street Journal* that a newspaper was a private enterprise "'affected' with no public interest" as "the most extreme formulation of the tory point of view with regard to the press" echoed sentiments that the president had also expressed. [24]

Reminiscent of the president, too, were the secretary's full-blooded attacks on columnists. In an article written in June 1939, one of Paul Mallon's attacks on him was described by Ickes as "a characteristic example of the sort of writing that has made him perhaps the least credible columnist in the United States." Mallon's technique, he wrote, "runs the whole gamut from mere insinuation to plain prevarication," the method being "to take a simple and in itself unimportant fact and weave around it a net of innuendoes, idle gossip, insinuation, juxtaposition, weasel words, and implausible lies." The upshot was a column "remarkable for its ill temper and mendacity." Having analyzed twenty-eight sentences in the article to which these comments related, Ickes concluded that there were, among them, nine "major falsehoods." [25] On another occasion Ickes described Arthur Krock as "the slyest and trickiest columnist of them all," and added that he was "also the most hypocritical, pretending a sobriety of judgment and a purity of motive that he does not possess." [26]

Nor did this indefatigable critic of the press hesitate to subject columnists to public ridicule. In a speech to the New York Newspaper Guild in April 1939, he referred to columnists as "that curious, endemic malady, which, in these modern days, has infected one newspaper after another," and mocked their pretentions in a poem which he recited to the gathering:

Wouldst know what's right and what is wrong?
Why birdies sing at break of dawn?
Ask the columnists.

Who run the earth and sun and moon?
Ask Thompson, Lawrence, Franklin, Broun,
Just the columnists . . . .

Who expound the Constitution,
Adding circum to locution?
Why, the columnists! . . .

When F.D.R. you want to sock,
Page Lippmann, Johnson, Kent or Krock,
Page a columnist.[27]

Yet, unlike Roosevelt, who objected to columnists per se, Ickes was
prepared to be discriminating in his criticism. "Of course," he wrote on
one occasion, "there are good columnists and bad ones...I do not
indict all columnists."[28] In contrast to Roosevelt, too, Ickes was prepared to give public recognition to the columnists' role: in the preface
to a collection of writings on the press, which he edited, he drew a
distinction between "calumnists," defined individually by him on
another occasion as "an ex-reporter who wastes good white space to
spread injurious gossip and disseminate prevarications and even unpublished libels," and "columnists," and observed that his criticism of
the former was not to be applied to columnists in general. "Many
columnists," ran the prefatory note, "who have replaced editorial
writers whose influence has generally waned, are high-minded individuals and fine commentators...[who]...worthily serve the public
welfare."[29] Franklin Roosevelt would not have said that.

Ickes displayed a similar willingness to discriminate in his attacks on
publishers, allowing that, just as there were desirable and undesirable
columnists, so were there desirable and undesirable owners. His disposition occasionally to praise sections of the press was also one which
Franklin Roosevelt did not noticeably share.[30]

Missing, too, from the Ickes' critique of the press were the constant
harping on the idea that, where they transgressed, reporters were under
orders from their employers to slant the news in an anti-administration
direction, and the intense concern over "interpretation" and over the
dire results such a practice would have, not only for the press as an
institution, but for the future of democracy itself.

In criticizing the press, Franklin Roosevelt, it is clear, was working within a larger frame of reference.

There is a further point: more than a suspicion exists that, far from being perturbed by the opposition of the press, Roosevelt actually welcomed it. Raymond Moley has recounted a two-hour "nightmarish conversation" with Roosevelt in April 1936, which left him (Moley) with "the harrowing intimation that Roosevelt was looking forward to nothing more than having his 'enemies'...reelect him." Numbered among these enemies, it is important to recognize, was the press. "Nothing would help him more," Moley has recalled the president saying, "than to have it known that the newspapers were all against him."[31] Others made similar observations. After interviewing Roosevelt at Hyde Park, James Kieran, in an article published in the *New York Times Magazine* on 3 October 1937, gave this interesting description of the president's decision-making procedure: "He looks at certain newspapers. If they are opposed to him, then he feels he must be generally correct. If they are with him, he becomes a bit suspicious." Similarly, Merriman Smith, White House correspondent for the United Press, has recalled that Roosevelt "finally got to the point where he seemed to relish the fact that the majority of the daily newspapers of the country opposed him politically."[32] Such an attitude was consistent with Roosevelt's indifference to press support where it was proffered, his minimization of it where it occurred, and his marked tendency to reject evidence, whether from his own newspaper reading, the Division of Press Intelligence, or other sources, which was inconsistent with certain basic propositions concerning the press to which he was wedded—as though the objective facts were irrelevant to his own perceptual field. The latter tendency was strikingly illustrated during a press conference on 23 August 1938, when, after he had designated 85 percent of the nation's press as "Tory" and therefore opposition press, a reporter drew his attention to a recent poll which had shown that three hundred out of eight hundred of the larger newspapers in the country supported the administration. His immediate response was an outright refusal to believe the figure.

Such an attitude was consistent, too, with an apparent disposition on the part of Roosevelt to anticipate or even to invent press opposition where it did not exist. It has been demonstrated, for example, that his Quarantine Speech was not, as Roosevelt implied, instantly assailed in the press as a whole,[33] a fact which must have been suggested to him by the reaction to the speech in the newspapers which he read each day, even had he not examined the breakdowns of editorial opinion on this question supplied by the Division of Press Intelligence; which leads to the paradoxical suggestion that, to some extent, it may have been the relative absence of press criticism of the proposal which the president found somewhat unnerving.

Thus, although Franklin Roosevelt repeatedly attacked the press for opposing him, the very opposition of which he complained was something which he was often able to contemplate not merely with equanimity, but with a degree of enthusiasm.

In summary, the emerging conclusions of this study are that Franklin Roosevelt persistently exaggerated the extent of press opposition which he faced and the extent to which calculated, proprietor-inspired distortion of news occurred; that he likewise exaggerated the extent to which newspaper owners opposed him, and, in his public statements at least, underestimated the degree of conflict which existed between himself and the working journalists; that his blanket condemnations of newspaper owners as a class and of newspaper columnists as a group are not easily reconciled with his relations with members of both these groups as individuals; that, in these and other ways, Franklin Roosevelt manifested toward the press as a whole an antagonism which was deep and fundamental; that, by inference, this antagonism was only partly related to the actual press treatment which he and his administration received; that, even allowing that the intensity of Roosevelt's antagonism toward the press may, to a considerable extent, have represented an understandably bitter reaction to the more virulent attacks on him, or the considerable opposition to his policies, or be explicable in narrow political or tactical terms, its nature is more difficult to account for in these ways; that, in this regard, Roosevelt appears to have possessed a highly circumscribed view of the role of the press, which its members understood with difficulty and shared with reluctance; and that, in relation to all these matters, Franklin Roosevelt's ideas and attitudes were stereotyped, inflexible, and resistant not merely to substantial revision, but even, over the period of his presidency, to detectable modification.

The tasks which remain are those of identifying the origins of the attitudes and opinions revealed or suggested by such conclusions; to reconcile, where it occurs, the apparently irreconcilable; to achieve, through such a reconciliation, a satisfactory and enlightening synthesis. What were the origins of Franklin Roosevelt's predominant attitudes toward the press? Why did he hold so resolutely to a series of propositions—about the extent of press opposition which he faced, about the nature of newspaper owners as a group—which he ought to have known were untenable? What was the source of his confidence when he lectured the press, his rage when he indiscriminately attacked it? Why, at times, was he gratified by its opposition, and indifferent to its support? What lay behind his severely limited conception of the role of the press, his curiously inconsistent attitude toward "interpretation," his deep-rooted and disproportionate hostility, which manifested itself so frequently and in so many ways?

The answers to such questions lie deeply embedded in Franklin Roosevelt's political philosophy.

Seven

Is a Jefferson on the Horizon?

On 3 December 1925, the *New York Evening World* carried a review of Claude G. Bowers' book *Jefferson and Hamilton*. The review was written by Franklin D. Roosevelt, and its tone was unrestrainedly enthusiastic. The value of Bowers' work, Roosevelt clearly implied, lay not in its originality, but in its relevance: its important message was one which he, himself, had sought to spread, when, in a recent letter to a thousand Democratic leaders, he had drawn attention to the distinction between the Jeffersonian and Hamiltonian ideals of government, and to the need to apply their fundamental differences to the contemporary policies of the two great political parties. But a suggestion thus advanced in seriousness had been greeted with derision; for, in their comments on his letter, many editors had "launched sneers at the mere suggestion that Jeffersonianism could, in any remote manner, bear upon the America of 1925." The memory of that rebuff rankled: he still boiled inwardly, the reviewer declared, when he thought of those "smug writers" who denied that "forces hostile to control of government by the people which existed in the crisis of 1790–1800 could still be a threat in our day and land." Under the circumstances, therefore, Bowers' book was a historically based rebuttal of the editors' criticism and an effective and timely vindication of Roosevelt's own ideas.

Having thus set the book firmly within the context of his own political beliefs, Roosevelt proceeded to call attention to some of the author's significant themes: to Bowers' depiction of Hamilton as an aristocrat, and a dedicated opponent of government by the people; to his depiction of Jefferson as the champion of the fundamental ideals of the Revolution; to his account of Hamilton's rise to supremacy, and, along with it, the control of the young government by "the moneyed class." Roosevelt went on to trace the growing division in the cabinet between the two men, with Jefferson distrusting Hamilton's liking for the chambers of commerce and his contempt for the views of the people, while Hamilton remained "confident of the power of his leaders among merchants and aristocrats," but was "wholly lacking in understanding...of...the average human being who...made up the mass of his countrymen." Roosevelt recounted, too, how Jefferson, in pursuance of his democratic goal, had begun "the mobilization of the masses against the autocracy of the few"—a daunting task, since, with Hamilton was aligned "the organized compact of forces of wealth, of birth, of commerce, of the press." After a decade of struggle Jefferson had finally triumphed: "His faith in mankind was vindicated; his appeal to the intelligence of the average man bore fruit; his conception of a democratic republic came true."

The reviewer concluded on a note of expectancy:

> I have a breathless feeling as I lay down this book...as I wonder if, a century and a quarter later, the same contending forces are not again mobilizing. Hamiltons we have today. Is a Jefferson on the horizon?

Although his depiction of Bowers' book as essentially a more fully researched and carefully spelled-out statement of his own political convictions was not entirely without foundation, Roosevelt's account of the relationship between his own ideas and those of Bowers is nevertheless unreliable. He had not, as he stated in his review of *Jefferson and Hamilton*, taken occasion, in the circular letter which he had sent to delegates to the recent Democratic Convention, "to refer in passing to the difference between the Jeffersonian and Hamiltonian ideals for an American method of government," and to the need to "apply their fundamental differences to present-day policies of our two great parties." His attempt, in that letter, to differentiate between the parties had been based, rather, on the simple assertion that, while the Republican leadership stood for conservativism, the Democrats must be committed to progress and liberal ideas.[1] The suggestion that the supposed differences between Jeffersonian and Hamiltonian ideals of government needed to be reemphasized and applied to contemporary politics was made not in Roosevelt's circular letter to the convention delegates on 5 December 1924, but in a letter to Senator J. Walsh, which purported to summarize the replies to that letter, and which, as part of a series of complicated maneuvers by Roosevelt and Louis Howe aimed at bringing about a national conference of Democrats, was released to the press on 8 March 1925. Referring to the replies which he had received from the delegates, Roosevelt had written in his letter to Walsh:

> My correspondents are overwhelmingly agreed that the Democracy must be unqualifiedly the Party representative of progress and liberal thought. *In other words, the clear line of demarkation which differentiated the political thought of Jefferson on the one side, and of Hamilton on the other, must be restored.* The Democracy must make it clear that it seeks primarily the good of the average citizen through the free rule of the whole electorate, as opposed to the Republican Party which seeks a mere moneyed prosperity of the nation through the control of government by a self-appointed aristocracy of wealth and of social and economic power (italics mine).[2]

But, clearly Roosevelt's notions that the Jeffersonian-Hamiltonian dichotomy needed to be reemphasized and applied to contemporary American politics were not "other words," a mere alternative formulation of the idea that the Democratic party should be the party of progress and liberal thought. On the contrary, in calling for such a political redefinition, Franklin Roosevelt had introduced into a letter, which otherwise consisted of a restatement of the thinly disguised program of party reform set out in his original circular letter, what had become, for him, a new and illuminating idea.

Although the precise origin of this idea in Roosevelt's own mind is uncertain, it is significant that several of the respondents to his circular letter invoked the name of Jefferson to sanction their suggestions on party reform, and that some delegates placed direct emphasis on the need for the Democratic party to reemphasize Jeffersonian principles. The closest approximation to the Jefferson-Hamilton theme, which Roosevelt, henceforth, would so enthusiastically espouse, came in a letter from M. W. Underwood of Michigan. This delegate called for the uniting of the Democratic party "in opposition to that class of our people who believe. . .that our Government should be controlled. . .by the few powerful financial interests, and special privilege [*sic*] class most of which have allied themselves with the Republican party." The government could be brought back to the people, the writer declared, only if "the historic Democratic party declare[d] its principles and what it stands for in plain and simple language, that the average man can understand." Candidates should therefore be selected who would carry out these principles, and, to this end, the writer suggested, "it might be well for them to review the life and policies of Jefferson[,] Jackson, Cleveland and Wilson for the purpose of learning the practical application of Democratic principles to Governmental action."[3] These ideas were similar to those subsequently expressed by Roosevelt in his letter to Walsh.

Even if the origins of his newfound political faith are uncertain, it is nevertheless clear that before 1925 Roosevelt did not adhere to its tenets, but that after 1925 he did. Roosevelt's political statements before 1925 evince little more than the blandness and insipidity of a vague progressivism. At his most platitudinous and politically vacuous, he told a Jefferson Day Dinner audience in April 1920, perhaps in a moment of self-revelation:

Never was there such confusion in the minds of the voters at large as to what the dominant parties stand for. . . . Let us not. . .forget the necessity of standing clearly. . .for something.

Then, addressing himself to the question of what that "something" might be, he recalled some advice he had given to a group of naval officers before the war:

My earnest word. . .is to urge you fearlessly to discard worship of all things that are old, and to adopt courageously anything that is new the moment that some new development of the present convinces you that the old way is no longer the right way.

"Gentlemen," Roosevelt told his audience, "I know of nothing better that I can say now than that."[4] It was a revealing admission.

Roosevelt's political ideas changed little between 1920 and 1924. In campaign speeches in 1920 he conceived of the political process in precisely the same terms as he was to do in his circular letter of December 1924—that is, as a struggle between "conservatives" and "liberals."[5] This was the simple theme, also, of a newspaper article which Louis Howe sent to Roosevelt in February 1924, an article described by Howe as "the best thing I have ever read and . . . *exactly along our lines of thought*" (italics mine).[6]

Unmistakable signs of Roosevelt's conversion to the idea that the essence of the political struggle was between the forces of Jeffersonianism and Hamiltonianism appeared, however, in 1925, not merely in his letter to Walsh, but also in correspondence with other political associates. Writing to Roosevelt in May of that year, Hollins N. Randolph, a lawyer of Atlanta, Georgia, referred to a request which Roosevelt had evidently made to him to write a comparative history of Hamilton and Jefferson. He agreed with Roosevelt, he said, that the present-day differences in principles between the Democratic and Republican parties derived from the philosophical differences between these two early political leaders. He accepted, too, Roosevelt's proposition that it would be helpful to Democrats who were trying to solve contemporary problems to adhere to the principles of government advocated by Thomas Jefferson. But he could not undertake the project.[7]

Under the circumstances, the enthusiasm with which Roosevelt greeted Claude Bowers' *Jefferson and Hamilton*, when it was published later that year, was understandable. Here was precisely the kind of book for which he had called in his letter to Randolph—a historical study which elaborated, in great detail, the rival conceptions of government which Roosevelt had come to believe were at the root of political conflict. Here, also, was a description of the first great battle for American democracy, of the alignment of opposing forces, of the organizational tactics employed. Bowers' book carried, too, the clear implication that the struggle which he so movingly had described had continuing relevance. To Franklin Roosevelt, to whom the book became a political bible and a blueprint for action, its publication seemed portentous, and his delight in its appearance was obviously unfeigned: "I felt like saying 'At last,'" he had begun his review, "as I read Mr. Claude G. Bowers' thrilling 'Jefferson and Hamilton.'" The book powerfully reinforced Roosevelt's emerging political ideas, clarifying his thinking and confirming his beliefs about the nature of political conflict. But, in all probability, it did more. For, in the skillful polemical hands of its author, the early struggle had not merely been depicted in ideological, but had been dramatized in personal terms—with the struggle between rival conceptions of government being reduced, in essence, to the struggle between their two major protagonists. "The spirits of Jefferson and Hamilton," Bowers had written in the conclusion to his work, "still stalk the ways of men—still fighting." Thus, for Franklin Roosevelt, when he read the book, the task became not merely one of persuading his party to adopt and espouse Jeffersonian principles, but of finding a leader who could embody them. "Is a Jefferson on the horizon?" he had asked at the conclusion of his review; but to that question, it may be imagined, he had already formulated a simple and alluring answer.

Nor was the point lost on Bowers, who wrote to Roosevelt of his delight at "the revelations of yourself" that appeared in the review.[8]

In a letter to D. C. Martin, written shortly after his review of Bowers' book, Roosevelt succinctly expressed the ideas which had become the core and which were, to a remarkable extent, to define the ambit of his political thinking.

We are approaching a period similar to that from 1790–1800 when Alexander Hamilton ran the federal government for the primary good of the chambers of commerce, the speculators and the inside ring of the national government. He was a fundamental believer in an autocracy of wealth and power—Jefferson brought the government back to the hands of the average voter, through insistence on fundamental principles, and the education of the average voter. We need a similar campaign of education today, and perhaps we shall find another Jefferson.[9]

Repeatedly, in speeches in the prepresidential period, he reemphasized these themes. "Thomas Jefferson," he informed a radio audience in April 1930, "represented a school of political thought, the principles of which are as applicable today as they were in the early days of the country." Jefferson had believed in "the rule of the majority," and had opposed "the minority...which sought to vest control of the new government solely in its own class." From the outset there had been "a sharp division in American political thought," and today, he and his listeners were confronted with "that same old conflict which Thomas Jefferson faced."[10]

Roosevelt's continuing commitment to the simple view of social and political conflict which he first elaborated in his letter to Walsh can be traced also through his relationship with Claude Bowers. Converted to Jeffersonianism while he was at school, Bowers' enthusiasm for the new faith must have equaled, and may even have surpassed, Roosevelt's own. Linked by their adherence to its simple, yet comprehensive propositions, the two became confidants and friends, and the tone of their correspondence makes it difficult to believe that Roosevelt's espousal of Jeffersonian ideas was undertaken merely for rhetorical purposes. When Bowers wrote to Roosevelt telling him of the growing success of his book, Roosevelt suggested that a cheaper edition might be produced and sold door-to-door, a system of distribution which, he told the author, was essentially Jeffersonian. Later, Roosevelt was to suggest that Bowers be included among the members of a special committee to be set up prior to the 1928 convention, so that the party might benefit from "his wonderful knowledge of. . .its historic traditions." Roosevelt enthusiastically welcomed the publication of Bowers' second major work, *The Tragic Era*, which interpreted the history of Reconstruction as the supplanting of a Jeffersonian Republic by a Hamiltonian one, and which, Bowers speculated, would bring electoral gains for the Democrats in the South. Roosevelt asked Bowers to deliver his nominating speech to the Democratic National Convention in 1932, and a discussion between the two of them of the style and content of the speech confirmed Bowers in his belief that the candidate was "a thorough Jeffersonian," who appeared, however, to show a liking for the methods of Jackson. During the campaign of that year, in editorials and speeches, Bowers was indefatigable in his efforts to explain the nature of the struggle which was taking place; after its successful conclusion, he offered a predictable interpretation of a campaign which, he wrote, was "as fundamental in its meaning as that of 1800."[11]

The same basic philosophy—the ideas which provided the bedrock political faith, which, underneath the flexible and opportunistic tactics which he so often employed, was never shaken—appeared in Franklin Roosevelt's discussions of American history. Although Roosevelt, as president, sometimes interpreted American history in terms of alternating periods of minority domination and majority control, it was more usual for his compressed histories of the Republic to be organized around a discussion of persons rather than periods. As it had been in Bowers' *Jefferson and Hamilton*, the struggle between opposing forces and ideas was epitomized in the conflicts between individuals, with past presidents being classified according to their attitude toward the crucial issue of whether the nature of government ought to be oligarchic or democratic. By these means, Roosevelt minimized the importance of political parties and boldly annexed to the Jeffersonian side the more revered Republican presidents: "I think it is time for us Democrats to claim Lincoln as one of our own," he had written to Bowers in April 1929. "The Republican party has certainly repudiated, first and last, everything he stood for."[12]

Roosevelt's presidential typology was elaborated in numerous speeches. In his Jackson Day Dinner Address in January 1938, he observed that the average American rarely thought of Jefferson or Jackson as Democrats, or of Lincoln or Theodore Roosevelt as Republicans, but that each of these presidents was evaluated in terms of his attitude toward the fundamental problems of government. All great presidents had believed in the right of self-government, and had had faith in the rule of the majority. Such men had recognized that, although the majority made mistakes, a small, privileged, minority, if it gained control of government, would unfailingly make worse mistakes, since it would not be responsive to the problems of all varieties of men. Such men recognized, too, that "in the long run the instincts of the common man...work out the best and safest balance for the common good." Roosevelt then proceeded to "talk history" to his audience, and to explain how successive Presidents—Jefferson, Jackson, and, more recently, Theodore Roosevelt and Woodrow Wilson—had each fought for what he referred to, with uncharacteristically ugly phraseology, as "the maintenance of the integrity of the morals of democracy."[13]

There is no question that Franklin Roosevelt, as president, saw

himself as being engaged in the same struggle that had confronted
earlier Jeffersonian presidents. In his Jackson Day Dinner Address, in
January 1938, he made this point explicitly when he told his audience:
"Once more the head of the Nation is working with all his might and
main to restore and to uphold the integrity of the morals of democracy—our heritage from the long line of national leadership—from
Jefferson to Wilson."[14] One consequence of such a view was that all
opposition to Roosevelt, whether from political antagonists, or the
Supreme Court, or even, he sometimes implied, foreign powers, was
classified and interpreted within this historical framework. Since the
applicability of his central ideas was universal ("The underlying issue
in *every political crisis in our history*," he told an election meeting in
October 1936, "has been between those who. . .have sought to exercise
the power of Government for the many and those. . .who have sought to
exercise the power of Government for the few" [italics mine]),[15] the
character of his opponents could never be in doubt.

It was the misfortune of the American press to be cast by Franklin
Roosevelt into the role of collaborator with the forces hostile to the
democratic control of America by its people. Why he originally designated the press as a Hamiltonian force is not clear, but, as before, the
replies to his circular letter of 1924 may have been crucial. Roosevelt's
statement, in that letter, that one of the fundamental truths on which
all the delegates would be agreed was that the publicizing of basic party
policy and the dissemination of current information ought greatly to be
increased, had provoked much comment. In the most impassioned of
the replies, Margaret Pike of Idaho complained that, apart from
occasional newspapers of limited circulation, the Democrats had no
press from New York to the Pacific Coast. Throughout the West and
the Middle West, the Republican press disseminated false and misleading information. The situation was likely to continue, declared the
writer, because business controlled both the press and the Republican
party.[16] To Roosevelt, who was, at this time, identifying the Republican
leadership with the Hamiltonian minority against which he was required to do battle, business and Republican domination of the press
may easily have been equated with Hamiltonian control.

Any disposition which Roosevelt had to see the press of America in an anti-Jeffersonian light would have been strengthened by the editorial reaction to his letter to Walsh, and, more particularly, to his suggestion that the differences between the original ideals of government needed to be reemphasized. The tone of some of the comments which Roosevelt collected was not merely unsympathetic, but scathing. "The Hamilton doctrines have been swallowed hook, bob, line and sinker by the Democratic party," observed the *Troy Times*. "Why lug in Jefferson?" Roosevelt's suggestions, declared the *New York Times*, in an editorial which the *Hudson Star* reproduced, are nothing more than "cheerful patter"; the Democratic party was "not likely to be strengthened by this sort of nonsense." In similar vein, the *Syracuse Post Standard* noted that the phrase "Jeffersonian principles" was "meaningless," and added unkindly: "Wait until the west learns that Mr. Roosevelt has his office in Wall Street!"[17] The fact that, as he put it in his review of Bowers' book, many editors had "launched sneers" at Roosevelt's renewed attempt to establish an ideological basis for party politics would not have encouraged him to believe that the press had changed its anti-Jeffersonian tune.

Other factors may have encouraged Roosevelt to include the press in the compact of forces which were opposing the restoration of the control of government to the people. The otherwise remarkable success of Hamiltonian minorities might have seemed implausible, his struggle against them too easy, without their assumed domination of the means of communication. Moreover, in the book which so profoundly influenced Roosevelt's thought, Claude Bowers had written that, in the first great struggle for American democracy, "the major portion of the press was either militantly Hamiltonian or indifferently democratic,"[18] an idea which was echoed in Roosevelt's review of Bowers' work.

From 1925, Roosevelt showed a continuing disposition to depict the press in ideologically hostile terms. "How can the good work [of organizing the Democratic party, as Jefferson had done, by disseminating facts] be reincarnated today," he inquired of Bowers, in December 1925, "when the Republicans own all the campaign chests and most of the newspapers?"[19] The same concern was expressed in important speeches, and especially in his address to the Democratic Victory Dinner at the Hotel Astor, New York City, on 14 January 1932. Those in the young nation, who had opposed Hamiltonian principles, had, he told his audience, been confronted by a serious obstacle: "the 'machinery of publicity' lay almost wholly in the hands of the conservative, privileged group—the political ancestors of the Republican leadership of today." To overcome that obstacle, Jefferson and his followers had been forced to organize a campaign to educate the people by disseminating information on the fundamentals of government.[20] Since he then proceeded to urge that a similar educative effort was once again necessary, the implication, so far as the American press was concerned, was clear: that institution was once more under Hamiltonian control. Similarly, in the compressed histories of the Republic, through which he sought, as president, to interpret the New Deal to the American people, Roosevelt was commonly to place the press on the side of those who had opposed the restoration of democratic control: against Jefferson were "almost all the newspapers and magazines of the day"; against Jackson, "all the nationally known press of the day, with the exception of three newspapers."[21]

Predisposed, as he was, to see the press, in simple aggregate terms, as a hostile force, Franklin Roosevelt's reaction to press opposition to the New Deal, when it developed during its first term, was predictable: such criticism confirmed his expectations regarding the press and established beyond doubt its antidemocratic orientation. Given his adherence to a rigid and intellectually circumscribed conception of the nature of political conflict, Roosevelt was not disposed to discriminate: evidence, whether from the Division of Press Intelligence, or from his own daily newspaper reading, which at times revealed a substantial level of press support, was resisted as irrelevant to his perceptual field; the hostility of some owners became the hostility of all; the faults of a minority were attributed to the majority. Nor could the opposition of the press have been considered by Roosevelt to be unusual or unexpected: if the press, traditionally, had been aligned against Jeffersonian presidents, could Roosevelt, now that he had come to take up the struggle, expect anything different? Or, it might be asked, could he tolerate anything different, since the opposition of the press, like the support of the people, confirmed his own presidential status? It is in this context that Raymond Moley's remark that "nothing would help him more than to have it known that the newspapers were all against him," and other indications that Roosevelt, at times, either welcomed press opposition or was indifferent to press support, take on particular significance. With the press against him, on the other hand, he could see himself fulfilling a historical destiny, standing as other great presidents had stood, against the Hamiltonian minority which once more threatened the American system of government. It was a scenario which was familiar, and deeply reassuring.

It is also within the context of Franklin Roosevelt's political philosophy that other puzzling aspects of his critique of the press fall more readily into place. That philosophy rested on a theory of human nature, which, categorizing mankind into a majority group and a minority group, attributed reasonable decency and democratic instincts to the former and unremitting selfishness and autocratic tendencies to the latter. At times, Roosevelt seemed to imply that the autocracy of Hamiltonians was congenital (in his review of Bowers' book he referred to Hamilton as "the natural aristocrat," and compared him with Jefferson, "the natural democrat"); more usually, however, he inferred that adoption of a belief in the rightness of minority control of government in their own interests was likely to occur in those who became wealthy and increasingly remote from ordinary citizens. It was a danger to which newspaper owners were particularly prone: "When the [newspaper] owner reaches a certain position of affluence..." he confided to Josephus Daniels, "he begins to associate with other Americans in the same rarefied upper brackets. He decreases his association with the little fellow, he begins to believe that the Hamiltonian theory was correct."[22] Roosevelt's conviction that most newspaper owners had actually embraced such minority views was made plain when he implied that most were Tories.

Erected on these conceptions about human nature was a theory of democratic government—a theory which postulated an essential role for himself, and a limited, yet vital, role for the press. Because Roosevelt believed that "the mass of humanity does think," that it could "make up its own mind on the pros and cons of all public questions," that it "often originates [policies]"; because he was confident, too, that "in the long run the instincts of the common man...work out the best and safest balance for the common good,"[23] he favored a governmental system based on the aggregate judgment of the many, rather than the selective wisdom of the few. (This belief in the superior wisdom of the many was described by Samuel Rosenman as one of Roosevelt's deepest convictions.)[24] In such a system, the people, reasonable and informed, initiated ideas or reached collective decisions; their representatives, sensing a demand for action, gave these ideas or decisions legislative form. In a radio address in October 1944, he drew a picture of such a system in action:

> The American people have gone through great national debates in the recent critical years. They were soul-searching debates. They reached from every city to every village and to every home. . . . As I look back, I am more and more certain that the decision *not* to bargain with the tyrants rose from the hearts and souls and sinews of the American people.[25]

It was a process which he contemplated with deep satisfaction and even with wonder. "It is amazing," he wrote to Carl Sandburg one month later, "that the independent voters of America—an increasing number of them—many of them without real education—do have that final ability to decide our fate and the country's fate 'in the deep silence of their own minds.'"[26] The statement recalled a sentence written fifteen years earlier in his review of Bowers' *Jefferson and Hamilton:* "Jefferson's faith in mankind was vindicated; his appeal to the intelligence of the average voter bore fruit."

Two of his own important functions within such a system were, he believed, to inculcate a knowledge of its fundamentals and to act as its informational hub. The educative function was one which, he believed, had been performed by all Jeffersonian leaders, and again and again Roosevelt was to make reference to his own efforts in this field and to celebrate their success. Thus, as his first term drew to a close, he declared that one of its two great achievements had been "the rebirth of the interest and understanding of a great citizenry in the problems of the Nation."[27] Similarly, on returning from a trip through the country in 1937, Roosevelt announced that his "outstanding impression" had been "the general understanding on the part of the average citizen of the broad objectives and policies" which he was about to recommend to the Extraordinary Session of Congress.[28] It was an impression which, Samuel Rosenman has written, gave Roosevelt particular pride, since he believed that his own fireside chats and other speeches had been responsible for the quickening of public interest.[29] Roosevelt was here celebrating the success of a program and a strategy which he had outlined as long ago as 1925 in his letter to Martin:

> Jefferson brought the government back to the hands of the average voter, through insistence on fundamental principles, and the education of the average voter. We need a similar campaign of education today.

His second vitally important function, which, like the first, had relevance to Roosevelt's expectations regarding the press, was to act, as he himself put it, as "the most important clearing house of information and ideas." He was required, he believed, to collect information from the people, to sift, refine, and interpret it, and to convey it again to them so that president and people could jointly reach decisions. The clearest expression of these ideas came in Roosevelt's Jackson Day Dinner Address in January 1940:

> Many years ago it had become clear to me that... the Presidency... could become the most important clearing house for the exchange of information and ideas, of facts and ideals, affecting the general welfare.
>   In practice, as you know, I have tried to follow out that concept. In the White House today we have built up a great mosaic of the state of the union from thousands of bits of information.

Then referring to his own cherished role as the nation's preeminently well-informed interpreter, he said:

> There is a deep satisfaction in pursuing the truth through the medley of information that reaches the White House, the overstatement, the half-truth, the glittering generality, the viewing-with-alarm, and, equally, the pointing-with-pride.... And there is the philosopher's satisfaction of trying to fit that particle of truth into the general scheme of things that are good and things that are bad for the people as a whole.[30]

This circulation of information between president and people was vital: "The constant free flow of communication among us—enabling the free interchange of ideas—forms," Roosevelt told a radio audience in October 1940, "the very blood stream of our nation."[31] Indeed, the success of the governmental system to which Roosevelt was committed was conditional on such an exchange taking place: "Jefferson realized," Roosevelt declared in January 1940, "that *if the people were free to get and discourse all the facts*, their composite judgment would be better than the judgment of a self-perpetuating few" (italics mine).[32]

In carrying out these perceived aspects of his presidential role, Roosevelt's identification with Thomas Jefferson, or, rather, with the Bowers-Roosevelt conception of Jefferson, was extraordinarily close. "I can picture the weeks on horseback," Roosevelt told a Jefferson Day Dinner audience in April 1932, "when he [Jefferson] was traveling into the different states of the Union, slowly and laboriously accumulating an understanding of the people...drinking in the needs of the people in every walk of life...giving to them an understanding of the essential principles of self-government." Jefferson, he declared, "knew at first hand every cross current of national and international life...[and] understood the yearnings and the lack of opportunity—the hopes and fears of millions."[33] It was necessary, said Roosevelt, in a fireside chat in October 1937, that "anyone charged with proposing or judging national policies should have first hand knowledge of the nation as a whole," which was why "again this year I have taken trips to all parts of the country." It was remarkable, he also observed after the same trip, how deep was the people's knowledge of their government and its objectives.[34] Roosevelt's sense of identification with Jefferson went further. He felt that, like America's third president, he enjoyed a relationship with the people which was intuitive. Of Thomas Jefferson, Claude Bowers had written, in the book of which Roosevelt so strongly approved:

He intuitively knew men.... In his understanding of mass psychology he had no equal. When a measure was passed or a policy adopted in Philadelphia, he knew the reactions in the woods of Georgia without waiting for letters and papers.[35]

Referring, at a press conference on 7 November 1934, to his conviction that the people were beginning to lose confidence in news reports because of the growing number of interpretative stories, Roosevelt told the reporters: "I have a sort of sixth sense about the public and they are beginning to lose it [confidence] more and more." This feeling of, in Frances Perkins' words, "being one with the people, of having no... barriers between him and them" was one which gave Roosevelt the most profound satisfaction.[36]

Shown, on one occasion, a pastel drawing by Kosciusko of Thomas Jefferson, Roosevelt was said by Arthur Krock to have been entranced by its resemblance to himself.[37] It was a predictable enough reaction from one who had modeled himself so closely on America's third president.

Just as the fundamental antagonism of Franklin Roosevelt toward the press, and his disposition to exaggerate the extent of its opposition, were outgrowths of his Jeffersonian political philosophy, so also were his highly circumscribed conception of the ideal role of that institution and the form which his critique of it characteristically assumed. Roosevelt believed that the mass of the people were naturally democratic, able to decide the great issues of the day provided that they were in possession of the requisite "factual" information, convictions which he thought of himself as sharing with Thomas Jefferson. "Jefferson believed," Roosevelt had reminded a radio audience in 1930, "that when the people were wholly informed on any issue, the decision of the majority would be right." "Jefferson realized," he repeated in 1940, "that if the people were free to get and discourse all the facts, their composite judgment would be better than the judgment of the self-perpetuating few."[38] As president, Roosevelt, who formed the center of a vast informational system, who was in constant, intimate (and intuitive) contact with the people, was manifestly the best source of the factual information on which the people, and, ultimately, the democratic system relied. If his obvious function was to provide such information, that of the press was to act as a vehicle for its transmission to the people. Though limited, the task which Roosevelt thus allotted to the press was therefore crucial. As Claude Bowers had written in the book which so strongly had influenced Roosevelt's thinking: "Believing

that the people in possession of the facts, would reach reasonable conclusions, he [Jefferson] considered newspapers as a necessary engine of
democracy.''[39]

Like this major task, the other functions which Roosevelt assigned to
the press were supportive and subsidiary: the press could contribute to
national debates and assist in disseminating a knowledge of the fundamentals of democratic government.

It was his conviction that the press was failing to perform such
functions, which increased his dissatisfaction with that institution and
compounded his resentment. By "slanting" news in accordance with
their own antidemocratic predilections, the press's Hamiltonian proprietors were obstructing the transmission of facts; by distorting or
ignoring his statements, they were hampering his efforts to spread
democratic knowledge. Jefferson, faced by a hostile press, had been
forced to undertake the colossal task of disseminating a knowledge of
the fundamentals of government to the people; Roosevelt, opposed by
the same force, had to embark on a similar campaign, which he
conducted over the radio and on his periodic trips through the United
States. In yet another respect the press was falling short. In theory,
newspapers could play a legitimate part in national debates, con-
tributing editorial ideas, stimulating discussion; in practice, because of
their established Hamiltonian character and the effective domination
of editors and working reporters by proprietors, they did not do so:
"Five years of fierce discussion and debate, five years of information
through the radio and the moving picture," Roosevelt declared in a
fireside chat in October 1937, "have taken the whole nation to school in
the nation's business"[40]—but the press was missing from the list of
institutions which had assisted in this process.

Against the background of Roosevelt's Jeffersonian assumptions
about human nature, about the ideal system of government, and about
his own role and that of the press within such a system, Franklin
Roosevelt's critique of the press can be comprehended. From his
conviction that if the people had free access to all the facts, their
composite judgment would be better than the judgment of the self-
perpetuating few, arose his insistent demand for straight, factual, even
literal reporting. "Write factually, truthfully, simply," he advised in

1938. "The American people are sufficiently intelligent, if given the facts, to draw their own conclusions—to form their own opinions"; "Do you think the ordinary. . .intelligent reader of a newspaper is in a position to. . .judge on a bare presentation of facts?" a reporter asked him at a press conference on 7 November 1934. "Pretty close to it," he answered, "yes"; "Give them," said he, "the facts and nothing else."[41] From his Jeffersonian assumptions about human nature and his related conception of the process by which national decisions ought to be reached, flowed, also, his antipathy toward the growing tendency to introduce "interpretation" into news reports. If "fact" was to be confused with "interpretation," a crucial informational link between president and people would be threatened, the system of government would be jeopardized, democracy itself might be at stake. That apprehension lay behind Roosevelt's letter to Henry Luce in 1940. "This is a form of journalism," he told the publisher, in a reference to the article which had inaccurately described the rather trivial election-night activities at Roosevelt's Hyde Park home, "which your President is perfectly willing to tell you he thinks of serious detriment to the future of successful democracy in the United States."[42]

Finally, from Roosevelt's perception of his own role as the most important clearinghouse for the exchange of information and ideas flowed his dissatisfaction with other interpreters of the nation's affairs—editorial writers and columnists—whose efforts he considered puerile on the one hand, preposterous on the other. Since he had "built up a great mosaic of the state of the union from thousands of bits of information," had pursued the truth through this "medley of information," and had attempted "to fit that particle of truth into the general scheme of things that are good and that are bad for the people as a whole," he, as president, was preeminently equipped to interpret the affairs of the nation.[43] He alone, as the people's representative, could take a truly national view. "I am," he told a group of newspaper editors at a press conference in April 1938, "more closely in touch with public opinion in the United States than any individual in this room. I have got a closer contact with more people." Because their business was "a local one," they could not "get a national picture" the way he could. "You cannot understand," he assured them, "no matter how hard you study the thing." And, he added comprehensively, "there is not a newspaperman that comes into my office that understands the ramifications of the national problems."[44] He made essentially similar criticisms of newspaper columnists, whose vision, based on incomplete information, he considered necessarily limited and distorted. Even Walter Lippmann, a serious writer, had "never let his mind travel west of the Hudson or north of the Harlem!" "I wish sometime," Roosevelt said of Lippmann on another occasion, "that he could come more into contact with the little fellow all over the country and see less of the big rich brother!"[45]

It is Franklin Roosevelt's Jeffersonianism which illuminates the more puzzling aspects of his relations with the press. Associated with that system of political and philosophical beliefs were his antagonism toward the press in general, his narrow conception of its role, his disposition to monitor it closely, to correct even trivial faults, his insistence on factual reporting, his hatred of interpretation, his antipathy toward correspondents, editors, and columnists, who, by interpreting and speculating, were impeding the flow of facts from the president to the people, and seeking to preempt his own role as the prime source of information for the people. Related to the ideological basis of his attitudes, moreover, were the general inflexibility of his views, the equanimity with which he sometimes regarded press opposition, his apparent indifference to proffered press support. Roosevelt's Jeffersonian beliefs help to explain, too, why he overestimated the opposition of the newspaper owners and underestimated the opposition of the correspondents, as he sought to make both conform to what were, to a degree, preconceived ideas as to what his relations with the press had to be; why, having associated the owners with finance ("the counting room") and wealth, he looked on them as being unfit to edit newspapers in the cause of democracy.

Roosevelt's commitment to Jeffersonian principles had a more practical outcome, for powerful ideological conviction, no less than superb political skill, strengthened his hand against his opponents. Just because his battles with the press were fought within a frame of historical and ideological reference which its members could only partly understand, and under rules which often they could but dimly perceive,

Franklin Roosevelt so often became, for that institution, such a formidable and baffling opponent; so that, in this way, Roosevelt's Jeffersonianism affected not merely the pattern of his relations with the press, but the results of his encounters with it.

In a comment on the outcome of those encounters Arthur Krock has written: "Genial, charming, shrewd and daring, he [Roosevelt] meets the press on his own ground and wins most of the battles."[46] The judgment is persuasive. As president, Franklin Roosevelt bound the reporters to him, winning their affection and offering them benefits too great to be ignored, and then flayed the press through them, using them again and again to strike at the newspaper owners; he enforced his rigid and often unrealistic standards, and used the press to get to the people, leaving the owners to protest, ineffectually, through their largely unread editorial columns.

Merriman Smith, White House correspondent for the United Press, once remarked:

> Mr. Roosevelt was good and he knew it. He was superbly confident that he was the best political strategist known in American history. He knew for a fact that he could outguess and outmaneuver his opponents. And he did, time and again.[47]

The press of America was no exception.

Notes

Preface

1. See, for example, Arthur M. Schlesinger, Jr., *The Age of Roosevelt*, vol. 2, *The Coming of the New Deal* (London: Heinemann, 1960), pp. 556-69; James MacGregor Burns, *Roosevelt: The Lion and the Fox* (London: Secker and Warburg, 1956), pp. 472-77; James MacGregor Burns, *Roosevelt: The Soldier of Freedom* (London: Weidenfeld and Nicolson, 1971), p. vii; Paul K. Conkin, *FDR and the Origins of the Welfare State* (New York: Thomas Y. Crowell Company, 1967), p. 99; Columbia University Oral History Project, Interview with Marquis Childs, 17 October 1957, pp. 50-51.

2. Burns, *Lion and Fox*, p. 473; Burns, *Soldier of Freedom*, p. vii.

Introduction

1. Samuel I. Rosenman, ed., *The Public Papers and Addresses of Franklin D. Roosevelt*, 5 vols. (New York: Random House, 1938), 2:38-39. Hereinafter cited as *PPA*.

2. FDR to Joseph Pulitzer, 2 November 1938. Franklin D. Roosevelt Papers as President, President's Personal File, 1933-45, Franklin D. Roosevelt Library, Hyde Park, N.Y. (hereinafter cited as PPF), file 2403.

3. FDR to Josephus Daniels, 28 September 1940, quoted in Carroll Kilpatrick, ed., *Roosevelt and Daniels: A Friendship in Politics* (Chapel Hill: University of North Carolina Press, 1952), p. 197.

Chapter One

1. Quoted in "Mr. Roosevelt 'Ungags' the Press," *Literary Digest* 114 (1933): 10, quoted in Leo C. Rosten, "President Roosevelt and the Washington Correspondents," *Public Opinion Quarterly* 1 (1937): 37; Russell Owen, "The White House Revolution Brought about by Roosevelt," *New York Times*, 19 March 1933, p. 41; Marlen Pew, "Shop Talk at Thirty," *Editor and Publisher*,

8 April 1933, p. 36, quoted in Rosten, "Washington Correspondents," p. 37.

2. Quoted in "New Deal for Press Praised by Henning," *Editor and Publisher*, 10 June 1933, p. 54.

3. Editorial, *Scoop*; see Harlee Branch to FDR, 14 December 1935, PPF 82.

4. Paul Y. Anderson, "Hoover and the Press," *Nation* 133 (1931): 382.

5. Walter Davenport, "The President and the Press," *Collier's* 115 (1945): 12.

6. Raymond Brandt, "The President's Press Conference," *Survey Graphic* 28 (1939): 448.

7. Marlen Pew, "Shop Talk at Thirty," *Editor and Publisher*, 28 February 1931, p. 70; quoted in "White House Corps Urged to Strike," *Editor and Publisher*, 18 August 1938, p. 22.

8. Rosten, "Washington Correspondents," pp. 39–40.

9. Ernest K. Lindley, *The Roosevelt Revolution: First Phase* (New York: Viking Press, 1933), p. 274.

10. Leo C. Rosten, *The Social Composition of the Washington Correspondents* (Chicago: University of Chicago Libraries, 1937), p. 7.

11. Bice Clemow, "Recovery on Way, Capital Corps Feels," *Editor and Publisher*, 29 December 1934, p. 8.

12. Quoted in Robert S. Mann, "Capital Corps No Propaganda Victims, Writers Tell Journalism Teachers," *Editor and Publisher*, 4 January 1936, p. 3.

13. Quotations from James E. Pollard, *The Presidents and the Press* (New York: Macmillan, 1947), p. 561; Clemow, "Recovery on Way," p. 8; William L. Rivers, *The Opinionmakers* (Boston: Beacon Press, 1965), p. 135.

14. Turner Catledge, "Federal Bureau for Press Urged," *New York Times*, 29 December 1936, p. 4; "Exclusive Set Gathers Capital News," *Literary Digest*, 6 March 1937, p. 28.

15. Jack Bell, *The Splendid Misery: A Study of the Presidency and Power Politics at Close Range* (London: T.V. Boardman and Company Limited, 1960), p. 180.

16. Davenport, "President and Press," p. 13.

17. A. Merriman Smith, *A President Is Many Men* (New York: Harper and Brothers, 1948), p. 157.

18. George H. Manning, "Capital Corps Hopes for New Deal," *Editor and Publisher*, 4 March 1933, p. 5.

19. Ray Tucker, "Secretary Early Helps Reporters," *New York World Telegram*, 8 March 1933.

20. Charles Michelson, *The Ghost Talks* (New York: G. P. Putnam's Sons, 1944), pp. 56–57.

21. James L. Wright, "Does President Pour out His Soul or Just Bunk?" *Buffalo Evening News*, n.d. For copy see memorandum of Stephen Early to Marguerite LeHand, 21 May 1935, PPF 82; Charles Hurd, *When the New Deal Was Young and Gay* (New York: Hawthorn Books, 1965), p. 230.

22. Arthur Krock, *Memoirs* (London: Cassell and Company, 1970), p. 183; Arthur Krock to Stephen Early, 16, 23, 26 February 1937, 1 March 1937, Early Papers, Arthur Krock folder; James M. Kieran to FDR, 9 September 1937, memorandum "G" (Grace Tully?) to "The P.S." (Marvin McIntyre?), 14 September 1937, PPF 392.

23. George Creel, *Rebel at Large: Recollections of Fifty Crowded Years* (New York: G. P. Putnam's Sons, 1947), pp. 289-92.

24. For correspondence between FDR and Anne MacCormick and Joseph Alsop see, respectively, PPF 675, PPF 300; Oiver R. Pilat, *Drew Pearson: An Unauthorized Biography* (New York: Harper's Magazine Press, 1973), pp. 34-36, 157.

25. The record of the Negro press's attempts to gain admission to Roosevelt's press conferences is contained in Franklin D. Roosevelt Papers as President, Official File, 1933-45, Franklin D. Roosevelt Library, Hyde Park, N.Y. (hereinafter cited as OF), file 36.

26. Frank L. Kluckhorn, "The Best Show in Washington," *New York Times Magazine*, 1 February 1942, p. 7.

27. "To Newsmen Who Know Dewey Best He's Not a Choice for Anything," *Guild Reporter*, 15 May 1944, p. 3.

28. Kluckhorn, "Best Show in Washington," p. 31.

29. Elmer E. Cornwell, Jr., "The Presidential Press Conference: A Study in Institutionalization," *Midwest Journal of Political Science* 9 (1960): 373; Elmer E. Cornwell, Jr., *Presidential Leadership of Public Opinion* (Bloomington: Indiana University Press, 1965), pp. 155-56.

30. H. G. Nicholas, "Roosevelt and Public Opinion," *Fortnightly* 63 (1945): 307-8.

31. Martin Gumpert, *First Papers* (New York: Duell, Sloan and Pearce, 1941), p. 301.

32. *New York Herald Tribune*, 26 October 1936, quoted in James F. Ragland, "Franklin D. Roosevelt and Public Opinion, 1933-1940" (Ph.D. diss., Stanford University, 1954), p. 456.

33. Gumpert, *First Papers*, pp. 288-89, 301.

34. Quoted in Clemow, "Recovery on Way," p. 8; Columbia University Oral History Project, Interviews with J. David Stern, December 1953-March 1954, p. 47; A. Merriman Smith, *Thank You, Mr. President* (New York: Harper Brothers, 1946), p. 22.

35. David Lawrence, "The Battle for the Headlines," *United States News* 5 (21 June 1937).

36. Cornwell, "Press Conference," p. 388; surveys chapter 5, pp. 169 ff.

37. Quoted in Davenport, "President and Press," 27 January 1945, p. 12.

38. Ibid., p. 46.

Chapter Two

1. Circulation figures for Kent and other columnists to be discussed are from Jane Turley, "A Study of the Syndicated Political Columnist in the Daily Newspapers" (M.A. thesis, University of Wisconsin, 1949), pp. 60-62, with the exception of those for Winchell and Franklin, which are from "Columnists and Calumnists," Secretary of Interior File, Columnists 1935-39, Ickes Papers, and those for Pearson and Allen, which are from Charles Fisher, *The Columnists* (New York: Howell, Soskin, Publishers, 1944), p. 216.

2. Eugene W. Goll, "Frank R. Kent's Opposition to Franklin D. Roosevelt and the New Deal," *Maryland Historical Magazine* 63 (1968): 158-71.

3. Jack Alexander, "He's Against," in John E. Drewry, ed., *Post Biographies of Famous Journalists* (Athens: University of Georgia Press, 1942), p. 364; Fisher, *The Columnists*, p. 191.

4. Quoted in "Columnists and Calumnists," *Guild Reporter*, 15 April 1936, p. 6.

5. David E. Weingast, "Walter Lippmann: A Content Analysis," *Public Opinion Quarterly* 14 (summer 1950): 297-302; PPF 2037.

6. Walter Winchell to FDR, 11 December 1933, memorandum Edwin M. Watson to FDR, 13 October 1941, OF 5547. See also PPF 5666.

7. Richard W. Steele, "The Pulse of the People: Franklin D. Roosevelt and the Gauging of American Public Opinion," *Journal of Contemporary History* 9 (1974): 200. For many reports from Carter (Jay Franklin) see Franklin D. Roosevelt Papers as President, President's Secretary File, 1933-45, Franklin Roosevelt Library, Hyde Park, New York, "J. F. Carter." Hereinafter cited as PSF.

8. Fisher, *The Columnists*, p. 216; Eugene A. Kelly, "Distorting the News," *American Mercury* 34 (1935): 312; Robert S. Allen to FDR, 19 October 1940, PPF 7112.

9. Fisher, *The Columnists*, pp. 290-91; Samuel I. Rosenman, *Working with Roosevelt* (New York: Harper Brothers, 1952), p. 247; OF 4818.

10. Joseph Alsop to Arthur Krock, 19 October 1939, Early Office File, Robert E. Kintner to Henry Morgenthau, 4 May 1939, Early Office File, Alsop Papers.

11. "Exclusive Set Gathers Washington News," *Literary Digest*, 6 March 1937, p. 29; Fisher, *The Columnists*, p. 127.

12. Lowell Mellett to FDR, 23 December 1944, FDR to Lowell Mellett, 28 December 1944, PSF, Mellett folder.

13. Arthur Krock, "Press vs. Government—A Warning," *Public Opinion Quarterly* 1 (1937): 45.

14. Columbia University Oral History Project, Interview with Arthur Krock, April 1950, p. 33.

15. "Communism Fifth Column, May 27, 1940," Raymond Clapper to Roy Howard, 29 November 1940, Notes on Discussion with Ickes over Luncheon, 29

December 1941, Clapper Papers, Diaries 1940–42; Columbia University Oral History Project, Interview with Arthur Krock, April 1950, p. 93; Krock, *Memoirs*, pp. 180–81.

16. Krock, *Memoirs*, pp. 180–81.

17. Arthur Krock, "Washington D.C.," in Hanson W. Baldwin, ed., *We Saw It Happen* (New York: Simon and Schuster, 1939), pp. 15–16; memorandum, William Hassett to Stephen Early, 28 April 1939, PPF 675; Columbia University Oral History Project, Interview with Arthur Krock, April 1950, pp. 42–44.

18. Smith, *Thank You, Mr. President*, p. 4; A. Merriman Smith, *A President Is Many Men* (New York: Harper and Brothers, 1948), p. 86.

19. Rosten, "Washington Correspondents," pp. 42–50.

20. "They Don't Laugh Just to Be Polite," *Literary Digest* 120 (1935): 26–27; James L. Wright, "Does President Pour out His Soul or Just Bunk?"

21. Kelly, "Distorting the News," pp. 313–14.

22. Ibid., p. 307.

23. Raymond Clapper, article in *Columbus Citizen*, 20 November 1933, quoted in Pollard, *Presidents and Press*, p. 813.

24. Krock, *Memoirs*, p. 182.

25. Rosten, *Social Composition*, pp. 9, 12–13.

26. Davenport, "President and Press," *Collier's* 115 (1945): 47.

27. Smith, *Thank You, Mr. President*, pp. 47–56.

28. Memorandum, Byron Price to Stephen Early, 30 September 1942, PPF 144; Robert E. Kennedy, "The President's Press Conference," *Chicago Times*, 7 October 1942; "Usual Banter Missing at Tense Press Conference," *Washington Star*, 2 October 1942.

29. Michael Reilly and William J. Slocum, *Reilly of the White House* (New York: Simon and Schuster, 1947), pp. 120–21; Paul Mallon, in *Boston Herald*, 16 August 1941, quoted in Pollard, *Presidents and Press*, p. 833.

30. Pollard, *Presidents and Press*, p. 833; Reilly, *Reilly of the White House*, p. 141.

31. Krock, *Memoirs*, p. 185; memorandum, Jonathan Daniels to Ruthjane Rumelt, 20 February 1945, OF 4695.

32. Hurd, *Young and Gay*, p. 228.

33. Krock, *Memoirs*, pp. 182, 186.

Chapter Three

1. FDR to Archibald MacLeish, 13 July 1942, PPF 245.

2. Quoted in Pollard, *Presidents and Press*, pp. 816–17.

3. Rodney P. Carlisle, "The Political Ideas and Influence of William Randolph Hearst, 1928–1936," (Ph.D. diss., University of California, 1966), pp. 77–79, 80–82; William Randolph Hearst to FDR, n.d., PPF 62.

4. Carlisle, "Political Ideas and Influence of Hearst," pp. 104–5, 108–9.

5. Robert R. McCormick to FDR, 6 May 1933, FDR to Robert R. McCormick, 16 May 1933, PPF 426; James Ragland, "Merchandisers of the First Amendment: Freedom and Responsibility of the Press in the Age of Roosevelt, 1933–1940," *Georgia Review* 16 (winter 1962): 367.

6. W. A. Swanberg, *Luce and His Empire* (New York: Charles Scribner's Sons, 1972), pp. 106–7, 131–32, 220; Robert T. Elson, *Time Inc.: The Intimate History of a Publishing Empire* (New York: Atheneum, 1968), p. 207.

7. For correspondence between FDR and Luce, on which this account is based, see PPF 3338.

8. For correspondence between FDR and Patterson, see PPF 245.

9. John Tebbel, *An American Dynasty: The Story of the McCormicks, Medills and Pattersons* (New York: Doubleday and Company, Inc., 1947), pp. 263–65.

10. Tully, *F.D.R. My Boss*, pp. 291–93; Tebbel, *American Dynasty*, p. 268.

11. For correspondence concerning FDR's relations with Howard see PPF 68, OF 53, and Early Papers, Roy Howard folder.

12. Roy Howard to Lowell Mellett, 26 May 1942, Mellett Papers, box 13, Roy Howard folder.

13. For correspondence between FDR and Ochs and Sulzberger see, respectively, PPF 29, PPF 675.

14. See below pp. 75–77.

15. For correspondence between FDR and Meyer, see PPF 5018.

16. See below pp. 75–77.

17. The correspondence between FDR and White on which this account is based is in White Papers, series C, boxes 217, 290, 320, and 347. See, also, PPF 1196.

18. Columbia University Oral History Project, Interview with J. David Stern, December 1953–March 1954, pp. 46, 48–50.

19. J. David Stern to Joseph F. Guffey, 6 February 1935, FDR to Marvin H. McIntyre, 4 March 1935, PPF 1039.

20. George Seldes, *Lords of the Press* (New York: Julian Messner, Inc., 1938), pp. 163–64; FDR to J. David Stern, 21 November 1944, J. David Stern to FDR, 28 November 1944, PPF 82.

21. Memorandum, Stephen Early to FDR, 23 July 1940, PPF 6646.

22. Marshall Field to FDR, 14 March 1942, PPF 6095.

Chapter Four

1. Press conference no. 661, 16 July 1940, *The Complete Presidential Press Conferences of Franklin D. Roosevelt*, 25 vols. (New York: DaCapo Press, 1972), 14:42. Hereinafter cited as PPC. See also *PPA*, 2:38–39; FDR to Norman Davis, 14 January 1936, quoted in Donald Day, ed., *Franklin D. Roosevelt's Own Story* (Boston: Little, Brown and Company, 1951), p. 257;

FDR to William E. Dodd, 5 August 1936, quoted in *Elliott Roosevelt*, ed., *The Roosevelt Letters*, 3 vols. (London: George G. Harrap and Co., Ltd., 1952), 3:605; FDR to Claude G. Bowers, n.d. (1937), quoted in Burns, *Lion and Fox*, p. 317; press conference no. 478, 23 August 1938, *PPC*, 12:41; press conference no. 649-A, 5 June 1940, *PPC*, 15:456.

2. See Marlen Pew, "Shop Talk at Thirty," *Editor and Publisher*, 26 September 1936, p. 48; J. Percy H. Johnson, ed., *Directory of Newspapers and Periodicals* (Philadelphia: N. W. Ayer and Son, 1941).

3. See "Gain in FDR Press Support Shown by Second E & P Survey," *Editor and Publisher*, 26 October 1940, p. 7; "60% of Dailies Support Dewey; Roosevelt Backed by 22%," *Editor and Publisher*, 4 November 1944, pp. 9, 68.

4. Frank Luther Mott, "Newspapers in Presidential Campaigns," *Public Opinion Quarterly* 8 (fall 1944): 359.

5. James S. Twohey Associates, "Analysis of Newspaper Opinion for Week Ending October 7, 1939," and "Analysis of Newspaper Opinion for Week Ending April 20, 1940." For copies, see OF 144.

6. See Carl Byoir to Marvin H. McIntyre, 7 October 1936, Early Papers, box 1.

7. Tully, *F.D.R. My Boss*, p. 76. According to Grace Tully, the newspapers which Roosevelt read each day were as follows: *New York Times, New York Herald Tribune, Chicago Tribune, Washington Post, Baltimore Sun, New York Journal American, Washington Times Herald, New York World Telegram, New York Sun, Washington Daily News,* and *Washington Evening Star.* The *Washington Daily News* and the *Washington Evening Star* are not available for research purposes: neither is listed in *Newspapers in Microform, United States, 1948-1972* (Washington, D.C.: Catalog Publications Division, Processing Department, Library of Congress, 1973) though the *Washington Evening Star* can be purchased from the Microfilming Corporation of America, Glen Rock, New Jersey. Grace Tully has revealed that, although Roosevelt had press clipping services available to him, he "preferred to make his own first screening of representative morning papers" (ibid.).

8. For representative sentences illustrative of the general tone of each of the editorials analyzed see Graham J. White, "Franklin D. Roosevelt and the American Press" (Ph.D. diss., University of Sydney, Australia, 1976), appendix A.

9. The editorial comments of the *Chicago Tribune, Washington Post,* and *New York Times* on the selected issues were classified by Dr. C. M. Campbell of the Department of History, University of Sydney, as well as by myself. Discrepancies are set out below:

Washington Post

	G.W.	C.C.
End of special session of Congress, 1933	GD	F
Congressional elections, 1934	GD	F

Invalidation of NRA, 1935	U	GD
Fourth-term nomination, 1944	GD	U
New York Times		
First Inaugural Address, 1933	F	GD
Congressional elections, 1934	GD	F
Fireside chat, 1938	GD	U
Destroyers for bases, 1940	GD	F
Election, 1940	GD	U
Annual Message, 1943	GD	F
Fourth-term nomination, 1944	GD	U

10. If the question of "weighting" is introduced, it becomes much more difficult to draw firm conclusions from the foregoing analysis. In his assessment of the strength of press opposition to his policies, Roosevelt may have been influenced by his knowledge of the relative circulations of the newspapers which he read each day, a subject about which he probably had general, though not precise, information. Thus, for example, opposition by the *Chicago Tribune*, which, in 1940, had a circulation of 1,076,866, would probably have weighed more heavily with Roosevelt than support by the *Washington Post*, with a circulation, in 1940, of 132,089. Similarly, support on a particular issue by the *New York World Telegram*, flagship of the Scripps-Howard fleet, would have been important, not merely in itself, but also because the editorial in question may have been reproduced by other Scripps-Howard newspapers (though this is by no means certain), or, if it were not, would probably have represented the general line which the editors in that newspaper chain would have been likely to follow. Similar comments would apply to editorials in the *New York Journal American*, a Hearst publication, and an opponent of the president. Further considerations arise. The qualitative importance of support by the *New York Times*, a not uncommon occurrence, would have been great, considering that newspaper's premier position in American journalism, its moral influence, and the nature of its readership. As, to the best of my knowledge, no satisfactory statistical method exists by which factors such as the ones referred to above may adequately be taken into account, I have decided to use a relatively simple method. The fact that the results of the survey of newspaper editorials correlate reasonably well with other evidence contained in this chapter, and particularly with the results of the analysis of the reports of the Division of Press Intelligence, suggests that the method adopted has validity. Circulation figures for the *Tribune* and the *Post* were taken from Johnson, ed., *Directory of Newspapers and Periodicals* (1941), pp. 1142, 1143.

11. For press intelligence bulletins see OF 1275.

12. Copies of the special reports of the Division of Press Intelligence are in OF 1275.

13. Memorandum, Stephen Early to Marvin H. McIntyre, 27 November 1934, OF 1275.

14. Memorandum on Editorial Reaction toward Aid for Allies, 1 May-1 June 1940, OF 788.

15. Lowell Mellett to FDR, 18 July 1941, FDR to Lowell Mellett, 21 July 1941, OF 788. All the weekly analyses to be discussed in the following pages are in OF 788.

16. See Lowell Mellett to FDR, 26 September 1941, OF 788, for Mellett's notification to the president of the change in the form of the weekly analyses.

17. Charles A. Churan to FDR, 6 November 1933, Harold F. Condon to FDR, 11 August 1936, PPF 426.

18. Louis Ruppel to FDR, 3 May 1935, FDR to Louis Ruppel, 9 May 1935, PPF 2133; see, for example, Lowell Mellett to FDR, 8 August 1941, PSF; FDR to William Allen White, 22 January 1934, 23 January 1940, White Papers, Series C, boxes 217, 347.

19. Rosenman, *Working with Roosevelt*, p. 99; Michelson, *The Ghost Talks*, p. 45; J. David Stern, *Memoirs of a Maverick Publisher* (New York: Simon and Schuster, 1962), p. 18; Hurd, *Young and Gay*, p. 238; letters from William O. Douglas, 23 October 1974 and Rexford G. Tugwell, 25 October 1974.

Chapter Five

1. William Allen White, Annual Address by President of Society, *Problems in Journalism: Proceedings of the American Society of Newspaper Editors*, 1939, p. 15.

2. White House Press Statement, 15 August 1935, PPF 62.

3. Quoted in Fisher, *The Columnists*, p. 129.

4. Memorandum, William D. Hassett to Stephen Early, 21 May 1940, Early Papers, box 2.

5. Quoted in Edwin Emery, "William Randolph Hearst: A Tentative Appraisal," in Edwin Emery and Edwin H. Ford, eds., *Highlights in the History of the American Press* (Minneapolis: University of Minnesota Press, 1954), p. 325; Paul Ward, "Farley Captures Labor," *Nation*, 31 October 1936, p. 512, quoted in Rosten, "Washington Correspondents," p. 51; quoted in Leo Rosten, *The Washington Correspondents* (New York: Harcourt, Brace and Company, 1937), p. 298.

6. John Tebbel, *The Life and Good Times of William Randolph Hearst* (New York: Dutton, 1952), pp. 169-71.

7. Quoted in Rosten, *Washington Correspondents*, p. 274.

8. W. Cameron Meyers, "The Chicago Newspaper Hoax in the '36 Election Campaign," *Journalism Quarterly* 37 (summer 1960): 356-64.

9. George H. Gallup, *The Gallup Poll: Public Opinion, 1935-1971*, 3 vols. (New York: Random House, 1972), 1:85, 120.

10. See chapter by George H. Gallup in Harold L. Ickes, ed., *Freedom of the Press Today: A Clinical Examination by Twenty-Eight Specialists* (New York: Vanguard Press, 1941), pp. 115-18.

11. Rosten, *Washington Correspondents*, pp. 220–25, 351–53.

12. Smith, *Thank You, Mr. President*, pp. 23, 25.

13. See Early Papers for these files.

14. Memorandum, FDR to Stephen Early, 20 April 1942, Early Papers, box 24.

15. Robert McLean to Stephen Early, 10 October 1938, Robert McLean to FDR, 10 October 1938, Stephen Early to Robert McLean, 11 October 1938, OF 171.

16. See PPF 426; PPF 62; Ellen M. Carmichael to FDR, 15 March 1942, Mellett Papers, White House 1942 folder.

17. See President's Diaries and Itineraries, PPF 1-0 (3).

18. Reporting by these three newspapers was examined also by Dr. C. M. Campbell of the Department of History in the University of Sydney. Differences occurred in relation to the reporting by the *New York Times* of the speech of 11 September 1940 (G.W., F; C.C., -M); the reporting by the *Washington Post* of the speech of 31 October 1936 (G.W., +M; C.C., F); and the reporting by the *Chicago Tribune* of the speech of 23 October 1936 (G.W., -S; C.C., F).

19. All reports for the *Washington Post, New York Times, New York Herald Tribune, Baltimore Sun, Chicago Tribune,* and *Washington Times Herald* appeared on the day following the press conferences to which they related; those for the *New York World Telegram, New York Journal American,* and *New York Sun* appeared on the same day.

20. The page-one reporting in the *Washington Post, Chicago Tribune,* and *New York Times* of the press conferences in question was graded independently by Dr. C. M. Campbell of the Department of History in the University of Sydney. Discrepancies are listed below:

Date of Press Conference	WP G.W.	C.C.
6 September 1940	F	-M
8 October 1940	F	-M
22 October 1940	F	-M
CT		
25 August 1936	F	-M
8 September 1936	-M	-S
NYT		
6 October 1936	F	+M
6 September 1940	-	+M
13 September 1940	-	F
1 October 1940	-	F
15 October 1940	F F	F -M

In the cases of the reports by the *New York Times* of the conferences held on 6 and 13 September and 1 October 1940, discrepancies were attributable to differences in opinion as to whether front-page stories on the following day were or were not based on press conference material.

Chapter Six

1. Roy Howard to Stephen Early, 9 August 1935, PPF 68.
2. Pollard, *Presidents and Press*, p. 799; Raymond Moley, *After Seven Years* (Lincoln: University of Nebraska Press, 1971), pp. 337–39.
3. William Allen White to FDR, 15 November 1939, White Papers, Series C, box 320.
4. Quoted in Pollard, *Presidents and Press*, pp. 817, 808.
5. *PPA*, 8:554–55.
6. *PPA*, 6:430; quoted in Pollard, *Presidents and Press*, p. 800.
7. See *Editor and Publisher*, 26 September 1936, p. 48, and 4 November 1944, p. 9; George W. Bain, "The Negro Press and the New Deal Alphabet Agencies, 1933–1938" (M.A. diss., University of Minnesota, 1966), p. 83.
8. Frank Luther Mott, "Newspapers in Presidential Campaigns," *Public Opinion Quarterly* 8 (fall 1944): 357.
9. Paul Anthony O'Rourke, Jr., "Liberal Journals and the New Deal" (Ph.D. diss., University of Notre Dame, 1969), pp. 206–7, 230–32.
10. Quoted in Pollard, *Presidents and Press*, p. 830.
11. Paul A. Porter to Stephen Early, 15 November 1944; Betty Wilson to Myrtle Bergheim, 29 November 1944; telegram, William D. Hassett to Stephen Early, 30 November 1944, PPF 82.
12. Memorandum, FDR to Stephen Early and Lowell Mellett, 20 August 1938, Early Papers, box 11.
13. *PPA*, 7:509.
14. *PPA*, 8:308–9.
15. William L. Rivers, *The Opinionmakers* (Boston: Beacon Press, 1965), pp. 42–43.
16. Quoted in John Luskin, *Lippmann, Liberty and the Press* (University, Ala.: University of Alabama Press, 1972), p. 94.
17. See News Clippings–Miscellaneous, FDR Papers, 1920–28; Ernest K. Lindley, *Franklin D. Roosevelt: A Career in Progressive Democracy* (New York: Blue Ribbon Books, Inc., 1931), p. 33.
18. FDR to editor, *Elmira Advertiser*, 10 June 1929; FDR to editor, *Lowville Democrat*, 14 May 1930; Attacks on Governor folder, FDR Private Correspondence, 1928–32.
19. Rosenman, *Working with Roosevelt*, p. 40.
20. Unsigned letter to editor, *Chicago Post*, 16 January 1931, Attacks on Governor folder, FDR Private Correspondence, 1928–32.
21. Memorandum, Stephen Early to Marvin H. McIntyre, 1 September 1942, PPF 675; memorandum, FDR to Stephen Early, 5 February 1943, PPF 6646.
22. Unsigned letter to Henry Luce, 20 November 1940, PPF 3338. On the basis of Roosevelt's draft, a lengthier but more moderate version of his criticisms was prepared by Lowell Mellett and William Hassett and sent, under the

former's signature, to Luce. See memorandum, FDR to Stephen Early, 3 December 1940, Lowell Mellett to Henry Luce, 7 December 1940, PPF 3338.

23. Elson, *Time Inc.*, p. 443.

24. Harold L. Ickes, *America's House of Lords* (New York: Harcourt, Brace, 1939), pp. viii, 10. Althought Ickes was only the nominal author of this book, both the research and writing having been done by Saul Padover, he would obviously have agreed with opinions published in his name. Authority for the statement that the book was written by Padover is a letter from him to me dated 9 July 1975.

25. Harold L. Ickes, "Paul Mallon's Propaganda Technique," Secretary of Interior File, Articles, 1939, Ickes Papers.

26. Memorandum, Harold L. Ickes to Saul Padover, 29 May 1939, Secretary of Interior File, Columnists, 1935–39, Ickes Papers.

27. See "Columnists and Calumnists," *Guild Reporter*, 15 April 1939, pp. 1, 6.

28. See typed sheets containing questions and answers to be used in Ickes' public debate with Frank Gannett, Secretary of Interior File, Columnists, 1935–39, Ickes Papers.

29. Ickes, "Columnists and Calumnists," *Guild Reporter*, 15 April 1939, p. 6; Ickes, ed., *Freedom of the Press Today*, pp. 12–13.

30. Ickes, *America's House of Lords*, p. vii; see, for example, Harold L. Ickes to John T. O'Rourke, 25 March 1939, Secretary of Interior File, Editorials, 1936–Family and Relations, 1940, Ickes Papers.

31. Moley, *After Seven Years*, pp. 337, 339.

32. A. Merriman Smith, *A President Is Many Men* (New York: Harper and Brothers, 1948), p. 92.

33. Travis B. Jacobs, "Roosevelt's 'Quarantine Speech,'" *Historian* 24 (1962): 483–502.

Chapter Seven

1. For copy of circular letter see FDR to Charles F. Murphy, 5 December 1924, FDR, General Political Correspondence, 1921–28, box 8, Alabama folder.

2. FDR to Thomas J. Walsh, 28 February 1925, FDR, General Political Correspondence, 1921–28, box 7, Walsh folder.

3. M. W. Underwood to FDR, 16 December 1924, FDR, General Political Correspondence, 1921–28, box 8, Michigan folder.

4. FDR, Speech at Jefferson Day Dinner, 10 April 1920, Speech File 116, PPF.

5. See FDR, Campaign Address, Chicago, 11 August 1920, Speech File 132, PPF; FDR, Final Preelection Statement, 31 October 1920, Speech File 233, PPF.

6. Memorandum, Louis Howe to FDR, 12 December 1924, FDR, General Political Correspondence, 1921-28, box 6. See article by Edmund C. Shields, "Democrat Says Party Needs a Sound Policy," enclosed with this memorandum.

7. Hollins N. Randolph to FDR, 4 May 1925, FDR, General Political Correspondence, 1921-28, box 6, Randolph folder.

8. Claude G. Bowers to FDR, 2 December 1925, FDR, Papers Pertaining to Family, Business, and Personal Affairs, 1882-1945, box 110, review of Bowers folder.

9. FDR to D. C. Martin, 9 December 1925, FDR, General Political Correspondence, 1921-28, box 4, Martin folder.

10. FDR, Radio Address to Thirty Luncheons in Honor of Thomas Jefferson, 12 April 1930, Speech File 374, PPF. See also Speech to Democratic State Convention, Syracuse, N.Y., 27 September 1926, Speech File 251; Speech Accepting Nomination for Governor, 16 October 1928, Speech File 261; Speech to Democratic State Committee, Albany, N.Y., 2 January 1929, Speech File 302; Address at Democratic Victory Dinner, Hotel Astor, New York City, 14 January 1932, Speech File 458; Address at Jefferson Day Dinner, St. Paul, Minnesota, 18 April 1932, Speech File 473. All in PPF.

11. Columbia University Oral History Project, Interview with Claude G. Bowers, 24 August 1954, p. 7; Claude G. Bowers to FDR, 19 January 1926 and FDR to Claude G. Bowers, 22 January 1926, FDR, Papers Pertaining to Family, Business, and Personal Affairs, 1882-1945, box 110, review of Bowers folder; Alfred B. Rollins, Jr., "The Political Education of Franklin Roosevelt: His Career in New York Politics, 1909-1928" (Ph.D. diss., Harvard University, 1953), pp. 803-4; Claude G. Bowers to FDR, 29 March, 6 and 18 August 1929, 17 February 1930, FDR, Papers as Governor, Private Correspondence, 1928-32, box 15, Bowers folder; and FDR to Claude G. Bowers, 3 April 1929, Bowers Papers; Columbia University Oral History Project, Interview with Claude G. Bowers, 24 August 1954, p. 89; Claude G. Bowers, "Aftermath Meditations," *New York Evening Journal*, 10 November 1932, Records of Democratic National Committee, 1932-33, box 861, Bowers folder. See other articles and speeches by Bowers at this location.

12. FDR to Claude G. Bowers, 3 April 1929, FDR, Papers as Governor, Private Correspondence, 1928-32, box 15, Bowers folder.

13. FDR, Address at Jackson Day Dinner, Washington, D.C., 8 January 1938, *PPA*, 7:38-41. See also Annual Message to Congress, 3 January 1936, *PPA*, 5:12-13; Address at Little Rock, Arkansas, 10 June 1936, *PPA*, 5:197-98; Address at Jackson Day Dinner, Washington, D.C., 7 January 1939, *PPA*, 8:62-68.

14. FDR, Address at Jackson Day Dinner, Washington, D.C., 8 January 1938, *PPA*, 7:44-45.

15. FDR, Campaign Address at Cleveland, Ohio, 16 October 1936, *PPA*, 5:502.

16. Margaret Pike to FDR, 17 January 1925, FDR, General Political Correspondence, 1921–28, Replies to FDR's Circular Letter, December 1924.

17. Editorials, *Troy Times*, 9 March 1925, *Hudson Star*, 26 March 1925, *Syracuse Post Standard*, 12 March 1925, FDR Papers, 1920–28, News Clippings, box 13.

18. Claude G. Bowers, *Jefferson and Hamilton: The Struggle for Democracy in America* (London: Constable and Company, 1925), p. 140.

19. FDR to Claude G. Bowers, 17 December 1925, Bowers Papers.

20. FDR, Address at Democratic Victory Dinner, Hotel Astor, New York City, 14 January 1932, Speech File 458, PPF.

21. FDR, Address at Jackson Day Dinner, Washington, D.C., 8 January 1938, *PPA*, 7:39–40. See also Address at Roanoke Island, N.C., 18 August 1937, *PPA*, 6:328–29; Address at Jackson Day Dinner, Washington, D.C., 8 January 1936, *PPA*, 5:40.

22. FDR to Josephus Daniels, 28 September 1940, quoted in Carroll Kilpatrick, ed., *Roosevelt and Daniels: A Friendship in Politics* (Chapel Hill: University of North Carolina Press, 1952), p. 197.

23. FDR, Campaign Address, Yonkers, N.Y., 1 November 1928, *PPA*, 1:69; FDR, Address at Jackson Day Dinner, Washington, D.C., 8 January 1938, *PPA*, 7:39.

24. Rosenman, *Working with Roosevelt*, p. 225.

25. FDR, Radio Address at Dinner of Foreign Policy Association, New York, 21 October 1944, *PPA*, 13:349.

26. FDR to Carl Sandburg, 3 December 1940, quoted in Manfred Landecker, *The President and Public Opinion* (Washington, D.C.: Public Affairs Press, 1968), p. 33.

27. FDR, Address at Jackson Day Dinner, Washington, D.C., 8 January 1936, *PPA*, 5:41.

28. FDR, "Fireside Chat" Discussing Legislation to be Recommended to the Extraordinary Session of the Congress, 12 October 1937, *PPA*, 6:430.

29. Rosenman, *Working with Roosevelt*, p. 171.

30. FDR, Address at Jackson Day Dinner, 8 January 1940, *PPA*, 9:31–32.

31. FDR, Radio Address to *New York Herald Tribune* Forum, 24 October 1940, *PPA*, 9:498.

32. FDR, Address at Jackson Day Dinner, 8 January 1940, *PPA*, 9:30.

33. FDR, Address at Jefferson Day Dinner, St. Paul, Minn., 18 April 1932, Speech File 473, PPF.

34. FDR, "Fireside Chat" Discussing Legislation to be Recommended to the Extraordinary Session of Congress, 12 October 1937, *PPA*, 6:430.

35. Bowers, *Jefferson and Hamilton*, p. 107.

36. Frances Perkins, *The Roosevelt I Knew* (New York: Viking Press, 1946), p. 72.

37. Columbia University Oral History Project, Interview with Arthur Krock, April 1950, pp. 45–46.

38. FDR, Radio Address to Thirty Luncheons in Honor of Thomas Jefferson, 12 April 1930, Speech File 374, PPF; see above p. 157.

39. Bowers, *Jefferson and Hamilton*, p. 108.

40. See above, p. 123.

41. FDR to Joseph Pulitzer, 2 November 1938, PPF 2403; see above pp. 45, 130.

42. See above, p. 134.

43. See above, p. 156.

44. See above, p. 130.

45. Quoted in John Luskin, *Lippmann, Liberty, and the Press* (University, Ala.: University of Alabama Press, 1972), p. 94; quoted in Arthur M. Schlesinger, Jr., *The Age of Roosevelt*, vol. 2, *The Coming of the New Deal* (London: Heinemann, 1960), p. 546.

46. "Arthur Krock Sees Threat to Press," *New York Times*, 8 October 1940, p. 12.

47. Smith, *Thank You, Mr. President*, p. 63.

Bibliographical Note

The basic record of Roosevelt's relations with the Washington press corps is contained in the *Complete Presidential Press Conferences of Franklin D. Roosevelt*, 25 vols. (New York: Da Capo Press, 1972), and in the writings of the Washington reporters, who regularly attended those meetings. The former is a register of the remarkably productive twelve-year dialogue between Roosevelt and the correspondents; the latter are found in rich profusion in contemporary periodical literature and daily newspaper columns.

The richest vein of evaluative comment on the president's dealings with the working press runs through the pages of *Editor and Publisher*, the leading trade journal of the newspaper industry. *Literary Digest* and the *Guild Reporter* frequently featured similar material. Among individual articles by Washington newsmen, Raymond Clapper's "Why Reporters Like Roosevelt," *Review of Reviews* (June 1934), is seminal; Eugene A. Kelly's "Distorting the News," *American Mercury* (34 [March 1935]), is an extreme example of the hostility which Roosevelt sometimes aroused; and Walter Davenport's "The Presidents and the Press," which appeared in *Collier's* on 27 January and 3 February 1945, capably sums up and synthesizes, near the end of Roosevelt's presidency, the views of the majority of the correspondents. An extensive sample of the many articles in the nation's daily newspapers on the president and the Washington press may be found in the scrapbooks of Stephen Early, which are among his papers in the Franklin D. Roosevelt Library.

A. Merriman Smith's *Thank You, Mr. President*, 2d ed. (New York: Harper Brothers, 1946) is an entertaining and perceptive commentary, by one of the nation's top reporters, on his news-gathering experiences in the period from 1940 to Roosevelt's death. Arthur Krock's *Memoirs* (London: Cassell and Company, 1970), and the interview with him in the Columbia University Oral History series contain acute judgments, by the president's most penetrating critic, about Roosevelt's relations with the press in the wider sense.

Of the literature produced by nonparticipants, Leo Rosten's account of Roosevelt's initial impact on the reporters and of the early foundations of his popularity with them, an account based on the writer's own extensive survey work among the Washington press, is unlikely ever to be bettered. Rosten's preliminary findings—"President Roosevelt and the Washington Correspondents," *Public Opinion Quarterly* (1 [January 1937]), and *The Social Composition of the Washington Correspondents* (Chicago: University of Chicago Libraries, 1937), were subsequently incorporated into his book *The Washington Correspondents* (New York: Harcourt, Brace and Co., 1937). James E. Pollard's *The Presidents and the Press* (New York: Macmillan, 1947), which carries Rosten's account through to 1945, breaks much valuable ground, though in basically descriptive fashion and without the benefit of the full press conference transcripts.

The story of Roosevelt's relations with the press owners can be pieced together from the correspondence between them and the president, which is contained in the Roosevelt and Early Papers in the Franklin D. Roosevelt Library, with the William Allen White Papers in the Library of Congress providing, in relation to that publisher, a rich and illuminating supplement.

It is in the press conference transcripts, too, that Franklin Roosevelt's controlling ideas about the press as an institution are made clear, though his basic critique is elaborated, also, directly in his private letters, and inferentially in his public pronouncements. Many of those public statements have been collected in Samuel I. Rosenman, ed., *The Public Papers and Addresses of Franklin D. Roosevelt*, 5 vols. (New York: Random House, 1938). Autobiographical writings by some of the president's close associates, notably Samuel Rosenman's *Working with Roosevelt* (New York: Harper Brothers, 1952) and Raymond Moley's *After Seven Years* (Lincoln: University of Nebraska Press, 1971), are useful in uncovering Roosevelt's basic attitudes toward the American press. The Papers of Harold L. Ickes, in the Library of Congress, contain much information on his relations with members of the press as well as the secretary's own vigorous and extended commentary on the press's performance and failings.

Many of the daily newspapers published during Roosevelt's presidency, including nine of the eleven which he read each day, have survived, and can be located through *Newspapers in Microform, United States, 1948-1972* (Washington, D.C.: Catalog Publications Division, Processing Department, Library of Congress, 1973). Additionally, the output of the American press may be sampled through an examination, in the Franklin D. Roosevelt Library, of the wonderfully detailed special and weekly reports of the Division of Press Intelligence (compiled, in the case of the latter, from a daily survey of four hundred newspapers), the many clippings which are to be found scattered throughout the Roosevelt and Early Papers, and the very extensive collections of press clippings in the President's Personal Book and the Stephen Early Scrapbooks.

The emergence of Franklin Roosevelt's political philosophy can be studied especially in his General Political Correspondence, 1921-28, and in the contents of his Speech File, both of which are among his papers in the Roosevelt Library. The constant reiteration, during the presidential period, of the ideas which Roosevelt had developed by the mid-1920s, may be observed in various documents included in the *Public Papers and Addresses*. The critically important alliance between Roosevelt and Claude Bowers is made clear in the record of the correspondence between them contained in the Roosevelt Papers and also in the Bowers Papers, which are held by the Lilly Library in Indiana University. Further evidence as to this relationship and its significance appears in Bowers' *My Life* (New York: Simon and Schuster, 1962) and in the interview with him in the Columbia University Oral History series.

For a much fuller list of relevant sources, see my "Franklin D. Roosevelt and the American Press" (Ph.D. diss., University of Sydney, Australia, 1976).

Index

Allen, Robert S., 30, 58
Alsop, Joseph, Jr., 18, 31, 50
Baltimore Sun: editorial attitude of, towards New Deal, 75, 76–77; reporting of Roosevelt's press conferences, 23, 109, 110, 112–13, 116; reporting of Roosevelt's speeches, 103, 104
Bowers, Claude G.: book by, reviewed by Roosevelt, 143–44; and Roosevelt, 147–48, 149, 152, 153, 157, 158–59
Chicago Tribune: editorial attitude of, towards New Deal, 51–52, 75, 76–77, 78, 89–90, 96–97; reporting of Roosevelt's press conferences, 109, 110, 113–14, 116; reporting of Roosevelt's speeches, 103, 106–8
Clapper, Raymond, 6, 8–9, 31, 33, 38, 95, 124
Coolidge, Calvin, 8
Creel, George, 17–18
Democratic National Committee, 72–73
Division of Press Intelligence, 79–89, 125–26; functions of, 79; press intelligence bulletins supplied by, 79–80; special reports of, 80–84; weekly reports of, 84–89
Early, Stephen, 59–60, 64; "Below the Belt" file, compiled by, 100;

influence of, on Roosevelt's relations with reporters, 14–16; obstruction by, of efforts of Negro reporters to attend press conferences, 8–9
Field, Marshall, 65
Franklin, Jay (John Franklin Carter), 30, 95
Grafton, Samuel, 30
Harding, Warren, 7
Hearst, William Randolph, 50–51, 94
Hearst press: public complaints about, sent to White House, 101; treatment of Roosevelt and New Deal by, 50–51, 89, 95–96
Hoover, Herbert, 6
Howard, Roy, 55–60, 121
Hurd, Charles, 46, 90, 111
Ickes, Harold L., 33: critique of press by, compared with Roosevelt's, 135–38
Johnson, General Hugh S., 27–28
Kent, Frank R., 27–28, 123
Kintner, Robert, 31, 50
Krock, Arthur, 10, 22, 136, 158, 162; analysis of reasons for conflict between administration and press by, 32–34; criticism of Roosevelt by, 38, 41, 44, 46, 122; exclusive interviews of Roosevelt by, 6–7
Lawrence, David, 23, 27, 28